OXFORDSHIRE COUNTRY WALKS

SOUTH CHILTERNS AND THAMES

GORING TO HENLEY

MARY WEBB   ALAN SPICER
ALLISTER SMITH

Illustrated by LOUISE SPICER

THE aRTISAN PRESS

The Artisan Press (Publishers) Limited

Cover photograph: Bluebells in a Chiltern beechwood
(Nigel Phillips)

PUBLISHER'S NOTE
The routes of the walks in this book all follow definitive rights of way
and have been checked by Oxfordshire County Council's Countryside
Service. It is advisable for walkers to use the latest edition of the
relevant Ordnance Survey Pathfinder Series 1:25000 scale maps to
follow the route of the walks. Diversions to the definitive right of
way may occur and walkers should look out for signs notifying
official diversions. Enquiries regarding rights of way should be
addressed to the Countryside Service, Oxfordshire County Council,
Holton, Oxford OX33 1QQ

Oxfordshire Country Walks – Vol. 6: South Chilterns and Thames
ISBN 0 9529238 2 3
First published in 1998 by The Artisan Press (Publishers) Ltd
Copyright © 1998 The Artisan Press (Publishers) Ltd

Typesetting and origination by The Artisan Press (Publishers) Ltd.
Printed by Information Press, Eynsham, Oxon

The Artisan Press (Publishers) Ltd
PO Box 1098, Winscombe, Bristol BS25 1DT
and The Studio, Sheep Street, Charlbury, Oxon OX7 3RR

Contents

Foreword

I came to live in South Oxfordshire nearly thirty years ago, and in that time have explored much of the varied countryside of this attractive area. An abiding memory is of an early visit to the Chilterns when I walked in the Aston Rowant Nature Reserve, at the time when the construction of the M40 Motorway was in progress.

The distress such developments cause to all who love the countryside, and the threat they symbolise for the future of a landscape for all to enjoy, were little heeded then, in an age when few influential voices questioned the wisdom of massive road building schemes. But the threats to the countryside, in South Oxfordshire as elsewhere, have not lessended; they continually appear in new forms.

Like me, readers of this little book value the countryside for the opportunities it provides for exercise and for refreshment, and wish to see it protected against damaging development so that future generations can continue to enjoy its gentle beauty. Explore this countryside while you may; use the footpaths and report any problems of access to the County Council; but don't forget that organisations like CPRE, working for its defence, need the support of people like you.

JOHN BEECH
Chairman, CPRE Oxfordshire Branch

If you would like to join CPRE you will find an application form at the back of this book. For further information please contact:

**CPRE Oxfordshire Branch, Freepost, Priestley's Loft,
The Barn House, Church Hanborough, Witney, Oxon OX8 8AB.
Telephone: 01993 883659**

CPRE

Your countryside – your voice

4

Preface

This series of walks covers the southern part of the Oxfordshire Chilterns, from an imaginary line between Wallingford and Henley-on-Thames to the River Thames which makes a large loop between these two towns. The walks cover both hills and river, including sections of the Thames Path long distance route.

The length of the walks varies from 5.5 to 7.5 miles (9-12km) but short cuts have been included where possible. There are some short steep climbs on most routes, given the nature of the terrain, but generally the going is good although expect some muddy patches in wet weather. The time taken will depend on the individual, but the walks are designed to be taken at a leisurely pace to allow plenty of time to read the descriptions and look at the landscape and wildlife. Ordnance Survey maps 1:25,000 will add to the interest of the routes and grid reference numbers head each section of the descriptions.

The guide has been produced with the aim of showing how much of our history, both natural and human, is present in the landscape. This part of the Chilterns has no large scale monuments. Instead the landscape records the lives of people from early man making flint tools beside the ancient route of the Thames, through medieval woodland clearances for agriculture, 16th and 17th century parkland, enclosure of commonland, the Victorian furniture industry and modern land use changes. The Introduction gives a brief background to the history of the landscape and the wildlife of the area.

Walking in the countryside is an enjoyable leisure activity but readers should be aware that all outdoor pursuits carry certain risks. The authors cannot accept responsibility for damage or injury to individuals or property occasioned by following the routes recommended in this book.

We hope you will enjoy discovering this landscape as much as we enjoyed producing this guide.

Introduction

The landscape of this area of the south Chilterns is a mosaic of woodland, agriculture and habitation, bordered to the south by the River Thames. This present day pattern overlies and often reflects an older system of land use which itself reflects the geology forming the foundation of all landscapes.

GEOLOGY

The basic skeleton of the Chilterns is Chalk, laid down during the Cretaceous period about 70 million years ago. Chalk is formed from the remains of microscopic marine algae which, over many thousands of years, were deposited as a thick layer at the bottom of a warm shallow sea. This bed rock is often covered with other deposits, which have either formed by weathering and erosion of the parent rock or by deposition from water or wind. Sandy or pebbly deposits (Reading Beds) were deposited after the chalk was formed during the Eocene period about 63 million years ago. Small areas of this material still remain, but the massive erosion which occurred during the Ice Age has amalgamated most of this material with clay.

Clay-with-flints is commonly found on the Chiltern plateau. Flint is very hard crystalline silica, usually dark in colour but often with a white surface layer where the silica has become porous. Experts disagree on the mechanics of flint formation. The clay is formed from residues left after the surface chalk slowly dissolved over thousands of years and from the remains of the Reading Bed deposits. The clay gradually mixed with flints which also weathered from the underlying chalk layer. This mixing took place during long freezing and thawing processes in the most recent Ice Age which ended about 12,000 years ago.

These various deposits have been used by people for many purposes. Flint is a very hard material, first used by early man for making tools of various kinds. The earliest date from 400,000 years ago, but there is evidence of flint being used in this way up to the Roman period. By striking the flint with another stone or a bone, razor sharp flakes are produced which were used for cutting. Further shaping of the flint would produce more elaborate tools such as hand axes, scrapers and knives. Since the early Middle Ages, flint has been used as a building material and is characteristic of the Chilterns, often combined with locally made bricks. There were many small deposits of clay suitable for brick making, such as at Stoke Row, although the major production area in this region was at Nettlebed.

In the south Chilterns, the proximity of the River Thames has also had an effect on the geology of the area. The river has changed channels over geological time and has left behind gravel terraces. Some mark the position of an earlier route known as the "Ancient Channel" of the river when it flowed more or less directly between

A Chilterns cottage

Caversham and Henley. Evidence of the earliest hunter-gatherers in the area has been found here, dating back to between 125,000 and 70,000BC. Other gravel terraces mark variations in the course and flow of the present river. Over time the river has worn deeper, so that the oldest gravel deposits are at a higher level than younger ones. The gravel deposits in this area are formed from flint derived from the Chalk and are now used for construction materials, the resulting pits filling with water after the gravel has been extracted. The river attracted early man along all its various routes, and the gravels are often a source of palaeolithic and later archaeological finds. However, it is thought that this gives a false picture of settlement patterns as there is a greater chance of archaeological finds where the ground is frequently disturbed as in gravel extraction.

Topography

The shape of the landscape is determined partly by the underlying geology but also by large scale earth movements in the distant past. The Chilterns were formed at the same time as the Alps, about 26 million years ago, by the collision of the continental plates of Africa and Europe. The Chalk strata tilted, rising gradually to the north west to the escarpment which looks out over the Oxfordshire Plain. The "Chiltern hills" are really a gently sloping plateau cut by a series of dry valleys, giving rise to the appearance of "hills". The valleys were cut during the Ice Age but have been dry in most cases for many centuries.

The open plateau with wide ranging views can be seen from many vantage points along the walks, the valleys often concealed from view. The contrast between the open tops and hidden valleys gives the Chilterns its special landscape quality. In the area covered by this book, the escarpment is not as steep as the distinct "edge" further north but instead is more varied with valleys and more gently sloping hills, so that sometimes it does not look like an escarpment at all (see Walk 1 Stoke Row). In the Thames valley the hills tend to rise from the river although there is sometimes a narrow floodplain close to the river (see Walks 3 Whitchurch, 4 Mapledurham, 8 Sonning Eye).

FACETS OF THE LANDSCAPE

The varied patterns of geology and land shape are overlain by another Chiltern characteristic, particularly in the south, the mosaic of woods and fields, punctuated by scattered villages and farms, linked by often narrow winding lanes. This landscape developed over many centuries as people gradually made best use of the land. The steep valleys and thick woodland did not encourage the formation of a more formal settlement pattern such as can be seen on the Oxfordshire plain. Despite this seeming isolation, the proximity of London has always provided a ready market for Chiltern produce, so from early days there was an interdependence between the two areas, although now only as a dormitory area for commuters.

Agricultural landscape

Before the coming of agriculture, the country was covered with woodland. Here in the Chilterns, the earliest cultivation took place on land with light soil such as chalk slopes and river valleys, leaving the heavier clay soils on the plateau with their woodland cover. This basic pattern continues to a greater or lesser extent today; notice how many woods are found on the plateau top.

During the Middle Ages more woodland was gradually cleared to increase land for cultivation. This process, called assarting, formed small irregular shaped fields, which can still be identified on modern 1:25000 Ordnance Survey maps. These fields were bordered by hedges, either formed from remnant strips of woodland or planted with woodland shrubs close to hand. These ancient hedges are still the norm in this area, although some more recent hawthorn hedges are found where commonland was enclosed in the 19th century (see

9

below). There were no large villages here, people lived in scattered hamlets, often called "End" or isolated farms on their cleared land which was surrounded by woods or heath. Again this pattern can still be seen easily on the modern maps and will be seen on many routes (Walk 3 Whitchurch, Walk 4 Mapledurham).

This landscape is a great contrast to that of the nearby Oxfordshire Plain where the easier terrain allowed cultivation in large open fields, only two or three for each village. These fields were divided into strips, each tenant holding land scattered between them. Each year the crops were rotated between the fields, one usually remaining fallow or unsown to rest the soil and clear it of weeds. This system remained more or less unchanged until the open fields were enclosed and divided amongst the major landowners of the village, between the 16th and 19th century, varying from place to place. The landscape became ordered with rectangular even sized fields, hedged with hawthorn. This landscape can still be seen from view points over the plain (Walk 1 Stoke Row).

The agriculture in the south Chilterns was arable; there was not enough water for cattle until recent times. From the early Middle Ages until the mid 19th century, the corn produced here was always of great importance to London. Crop rotations were operated as in the open fields, but because smaller land units were involved, this system could be more flexible. Sheep, which do not require as much water as cattle, were allied to arable production and were used for their manuring capabilities as well as for wool or meat. Although seemingly isolated and perhaps rather primitive, during the 13th century this area was one of the first to change from oxen to horses for ploughing, partly because they were able to work more easily and faster in the smaller fields and could also be used for other jobs.

New crops, such as clovers and turnips, were introduced during the 17th and 18th centuries, and mechanisation in the early 20th century, but in general the fieldscape changed little for several centuries. After the Second World War and the drive to be nationally self-sufficient in food, large agricultural machinery became widely used resulting in hedges being removed to make room for them, particularly on the flatter land. New crops and methods have been introduced, changing the landscape on a seasonal basis. The yellow of oil seed rape and the blue of flax is a common sight, as are the green winter fields of autumn sown crops, a marked change from the bare earth of the recent past. However, in many places, today's agricultural landscape can still be identified on maps made two hundred years ago.

Cherry growing had a long tradition in the Chilterns, the fruit being used for pies and making alcoholic drinks as well as fresh fruit. Around Stoke Row and Woodcote evidence of this can still be seen, and wild cherry trees are a feature of the woods, especially in spring when the blossom is in flower.

Wooded landscape

In the past, the woodland contained many different tree species, although beech was one of the most common. Much of the woodland was coppiced, trees being cut to ground level to produce new growth over a cycle of years. The main use for most of the wood produced by coppicing was for fire wood, much being taken by river to London, as well as to Oxford and the Vale of Aylesbury for many centuries. It was also used in brick kilns and in glassmaking at Henley and other local places.

By the end of the 18th century, cheap coal transported by canal was reducing the trade in coppice wood. A new use was found for the small timber from coppice, namely the making of chair parts for Windsor chairs. Legs, backs and stretchers were turned on pole lathes by bodgers, men working and living in the woods. Beech was ideal for this trade as it is the only wood which can be turned in its green state. Ash was used for the bows forming the back of the chairs, and elm for the seats, both woods plentiful in the area at that time. Gradually the chair making industry became locally widespread, High Wycombe becoming the main industrial centre by the mid 19th century, but with many small workshops throughout the southern Chilterns (see Walk 1 Stoke Row). Trees were felled at different ages and sizes depending on the user, local bodger or industrialised chair factory, but gradually beech was deliberately planted as a timber tree where areas were cleared and replanted, and the woods became the high forest we see today. Coppicing mostly died out, the large logs being split into smaller billet suitable for turning. The only evidence today of this past activity are the numerous saw pits still to be found in most woods, now oval hollows often filled with dead leaves. When in use, the pits were much larger and had a timber frame over them. Two men used to work in the pit, using a two man saw to cut the logs into planks. The top dog made the downward cut stroke while the under dog guided the saw down and made the upward stroke. This continued into the 20th century until steam power enabled logs to be removed whole and cut up in steam powered sawmills.

Commons – little known landscape

Although the beech woods are thought of as the typical landscape characteristic of the Chilterns, amongst the pattern of woods and fields were large areas of common heathland or "waste". These areas of heath developed on the poorer soils with sand and pebbles, often on the Reading Beds (see Geology) which were no use for agriculture. Thin grasses, bracken, heather and gorse grew there as well as scattered trees and shrubs, which were often pollarded, cut to a height above the reach of grazing animals and allowed to regrow in the same way as coppiced trees. The straggling shaped commons often became funnel shaped, the land narrowing to a point, where roads left the commonland.

The land was owned by the Lord of the Manor but people had common rights, often linked to their habitation, which allowed them to graze their animals, collect furze (gorse) or fallen timber (estovers) for fuel, and take minerals such as clay and sand, often leading to the development of brick kilns on the commons. Commons were usually marked by a bank which would

12

have been topped by a fence or other barrier to keep grazing animals out of fields or private woods. The bank also showed where the common rights were allowed. Some woods were also "common", again used for grazing and estovers, although the Lord of the Manor owned the wood and timber. Again pollarded trees were frequent and old pollards can still be seen in areas of old common woodland. Maps such as that made by Richard Davis in 1797 show the commons as rough land, very different from the ordered arable fields or managed woods, indicating them to be the last untamed areas in the region.

The edges of commons were sometimes encroached upon by people who built cottages, usually illegally, and the increase in this practice led eventually to many commons being enclosed by Acts of Parliament, especially during the first half of the 19th century. The land was divided amongst the people who had common rights, but invariably the large landowners shared the bulk of the land. Some of the later Enclosure Awards provided "allotments" – land allotted to the poor so that they could grow vegetables or keep a pig and chickens, whilst other provision was made to keep some of the common for recreation. Schools and cemeteries were also often planned at the same time. The remaining ex-common land was divided up into regular rectangular fields, obvious on an Ordnance Survey map amongst the more irregular shaped older fields. Although it was hoped that the land was suitable for agriculture with more modern techniques, it was often found to be still worthless for farming. Gradually much of this land was sold for housing, and many settlements fit well into the old shape of the previous commonland (see Walks 2 Woodcote, 5 Peppard Common and Kingwood Common, 6 Rotherfield Peppard and Crowsley). For various reasons, not all the commonland was enclosed, and these can still be seen at Rotherfield Peppard and Kingwood. Despite the passage of time and changes in use having altered their appearance, it is still possible to imagine the landscape of the old commons interspersed amongst the fields and woods.

TRANSPORT
AND THE LANDSCAPE

Although some roads in this area are busy, carrying traffic to Reading from Wallingford or Henley, most are quiet lanes or tracks. Some roads are quite recent, having been set out as a result of the Parliamentary Enclosures of the commons at Woodcote and Goring Heath. Most routes, however, are ancient; they evolved as people travelled between farms and hamlets or to river crossings. They often run between steep flint or chalk banks or ancient mixed species hedges and are little changed from pre-car days. Pub names like the Pack Horse and Pack Saddle indicate that wheeled traffic was once rare. Old maps show most routes to be of equal importance, but today many are nothing more than rough tracks or footpaths, with surfaces probably similar to those in the past.

Some routes led up to areas of common grazing away from the main settlements. Many of the ancient parishes were "strip parishes", long and narrow, stretching from the river up into the hills so that each parish had a share of different types of land and conditions. The better agricultural land was closer to the river with woodland and grazing on the rough commonland in the hills. Many old tracks reflect this, showing how people travelled between different parts of the parish, herding their flocks of sheep to and from common grazing or carrying wood down to the settlement or the river. Some historical parish boundaries have changed as new parishes including Woodcote, Goring Heath, and Sonning Common were formed when the large tracts of commonland were enclosed in the 19th century so breaking this old pattern in some places.

Some of these quiet lanes had specific roles to play. The winter route of the Icknield Way – the Chiltern Ridgeway – followed the crest of the Chiltern escarpment and we cross a section of this during Walk 2 Stoke Row. The Icknield Way is thought to be one of the oldest routes in England, linking Wessex and East Anglia since Neolithic times, between 4,000 to 2,000 BC. Its name comes from that of the Iceni, a later tribe, to whose territory it led. This was not a formal track, but one followed as part of a wide belt of transit, along the Chiltern escarpment long before fields and lanes were formed. Over time, the route became more formalised with varying routes taken according to the ground conditions at different seasons, of which the Upper and Lower Icknield Way are most obvious today. The Lower Icknield Way was improved by the Romans, and both were used as drove roads until the 19th century when they were reduced to bridleways by the Enclosure Acts. The Upper Icknield Way is now part of the Ridgeway Long Distance Path. The third route along the top of the Chilterns is less obvious, but can be traced along paths and lanes; some historians call this the summer route, others the winter route. It would have followed the line of drier chalk in the winter but would also have been acceptable in summer when the clay capping the chalk is baked hard by the sun.

Another interesting route is the "short cut" between Goring and Henley-on-Thames where river-borne goods were moved by packhorse rather than by boat round the long bend of the river between these two towns (see Walks 2 Woodcote 5 Peppard Common and Kingwood Common). Goods were unloaded from barges and taken by road because of the difficulties encountered in navigating the river here (see below).

River Thames

The River Thames was a major route for goods in both directions between London and Henley during the Middle Ages. Earlier the river had been navigable to Oxford, but the increase in the number of water mills and the weirs needed to supply adequate water to them, made this very difficult so by the latter part of the 13th century Henley was the highest navigable point. Eventually improvements were made and the river was opened to Oxford in 1635, but the going was still slow with shallow water and primitive locks often causing barges to ground, hence the use of the pack-horse short cut (see above). By the time the Thames was improved with new locks, it had been overtaken by the new canals and railways. Traditionally, wood for fuel, building stone, and corn were major items bound for London. Luxury goods, and later coal, returned up stream, particularly to the large houses and estates bordering the river.

The river today is used by pleasure craft, either for sport or leisure. Henley was the site for the first Oxford and Cambridge Boat Race held in 1829 and won by Oxford. Today the Oxford crew often train between Henley and Wallingford. The world famous Henley Royal Regatta has been staged there since 1839. Other craft are holiday boats, rather more luxurious than the rowing boat and canvas cover used by Jerome K. Jerome's "Three Men in a Boat"!

Railway

The river valley forms a natural cutting between the Chilterns and the Berkshire Downs so this was the obvious place for a railway route west from London to Bristol. Originally part of the Great Western Railway, the line was designed by Isambard Kingdom Brunel and opened in 1840.

Air

Today's walkers cannot help but be aware of another transport corridor, this time overhead as planes from Heathrow Airport travel westwards. The most marked of these is the daily Concorde flight which at the time of writing is overhead at about 10.50am. Although it is noisy, it is nevertheless a spectacular sight but will soon be as much a part of history as are barges on the Thames.

NATURAL HISTORY

As elsewhere in England, wildlife in the Chilterns has been diminished by high intensity agriculture and the spread of urbanisation. This area has a rich variety of wildlife in a wide range of habitats but most of these are fragmented and diminishing. Action is needed to

Red kite

maintain the species diversity of heathland, old woodland, river plain wetlands and unimproved grasslands. A Biodiversity Challenge has recently been launched by BBONT (Berkshire, Buckinghamshire and Oxfordshire Naturalists' Trust) and other similar groups to encourage conservation action to enhance the wildlife of the area. A very successful project, which predated this initiative, was the re-introduction by the Royal Society for the Protection of Birds and English Nature of the red kite, a spectacular bird with a distinctive forked tail and reddish plumage which you may well see in the area covered by these walks.

Heathland and Commons

In the past, quite large areas of the south Chilterns were covered with heather, bracken, gorse and acid tolerant grasses growing on the heaths and commons. Since the Second World War, most of the remaining commonland has been invaded by birch and scrub which has led to a disappearance or decline in typical species such as nightjar, nightingale and adder. This is a rare habitat throughout lowland Europe and only 0.001% of land

Nightjar

with high nature conservation value in Oxfordshire is lowland heath, so it is an extremely important habitat. There is now an active project to restore some of these neglected heaths in this area. In 1993 the Nettlebed and District Commons Conservators, who administer Kingwood Common, Peppard Common and others, joined with BBONT and the Countryside Commission to restore and extend parts of the surviving heathland and maintain the glades and woodland rides (see Walk 5 Peppard Common and Kingwood Common).

Woodlands

Many of the woods in this area are ancient, the land having been covered by trees for many centuries, although the appearance has changed, altered by human management of the woodland for different resources as described above. Ancient woodland contains a particular group of plants which thrive in the shady conditions. They are slow growing and spread very slowly so are evidence of long continuity of woodland cover. Species such as sanicle, wood anemone, wood sorrel, goldilocks buttercup, woodruff, wood spurge and spurge laurel are frequently seen indicator species; there are many other less common species. In order to positively identify ancient woodland several indicators have to be present along with other clues such as map or documentary evidence.

Nuthatch (left) and treecreeper

The living trees harbour many kinds of insects, but decaying wood also provides a habitat for an equally rich but different variety of insects. Wood boring beetles, wasps and bees, together with fungi soften the dead timber providing shelter and food for myriads of woodlice, spiders, flies and worms. This

18

represents a plentiful supply of food for birds such as woodpeckers, nuthatches and tree creepers found in the Chiltern woods. Holes and crevices in dead or dying trees provide nest and roost sites for these birds as well as for owls, kestrels, tits, wrens and bats. The nuts of hazel, beech, oak and sweet chestnut feed nuthatches, jays, squirrels, dormice and other mice. Dormice need low scrub for their summer breeding nests; hazel coppice is particularly suitable. However, this type of woodland management has mostly died out except on some conservation sites but a BBONT survey is currently under way to estimate the numbers of these animals in the Chilterns.

Broadleaf secondary woodland, arising from replanting or regeneration on sites of cleared ancient woods, are also important for their insect populations. Such woods contain birch, willow, aspen and blackthorn, all attracting insects to their seeds and flowers. Even conifers, particularly Scots pine, have their own insect fauna and the evergreen foliage provides year round shelter and nest sites for many birds, especially the goldcrest, Britain's smallest bird.

Goldcrest

Hedgerows

Many of the hedges you will come across on these walks are remnants of old woodland, left after clearing land for agriculture and used as a boundary or a barrier; some of these are likely to be very old. If they are woodland remnants, indicator plants as described earlier may be present in the hedge bottom. Some originated as boundaries for parishes, commonland, or historic manors and estates. Others have been planted, usually with hawthorn, when commons were enclosed to make arable fields for crops or pasture for stock.

Hedges may contain protected or endangered birds, animals or plants or rich mixtures of trees and shrubs. They often also act as an historical record showing changes to the landscape, and by their composition can help to date these events. Legislation was introduced in 1997 to protect hedges of wildlife or historic importance. The Oxfordshire branch of the CPRE (Council for the Protection of Rural England) has developed a county-wide scheme to survey important hedges. It is working closely with Oxfordshire County Council's Biological Record Centre to ensure protection of these important landscape features.

Chalk grassland

Unimproved chalk grassland with its rich diversity of alkaline tolerant flowering plants, blue butterflies, moths and grasshoppers is now rare in this area. In the past, the Chilterns plateau and scarp were covered with a mosaic of woodland and downland, often grazed as commonland. This habitat took many centuries to evolve; the plant communities developed in response to the lack of competition from tall grasses which cannot thrive when grazed by animals, or in poor soil and dry conditions. This habitat is a last refuge for many plants and associated insects, which cannot survive elsewhere. Now much of this grassland has either scrubbed over, since grazing declined and the rabbit population was drastically reduced by myxomatosis, or has been converted to lush grass, but flower deficient pastures by use of herbicides and fertilizers.

Small areas of rich chalk grasslands still remain on steep slopes at the edge of the Thames valley as seen at Hartslock Nature Reserve (Walk 3) and at Mapledurham (Walk 4) where the land has not been modified. Other remnants may be seen in landscaped parkland at Crowsley (Walk 6) or in the verges of old tracks as at Dunsden (Walk 8).

River and wetlands

Much of the floodplain of the Thames in this area has been drained and converted to pasture treated with pesticides and artificial fertilizers. Large scale gravel extraction at Sonning and urban developments at Reading, Caversham and Pangbourne have destroyed much of the former marshy land. Remnants as at Shiplake (Walk 8) contain reeds, sedges and attractive wetland plants including meadowsweet, valerian, meadow rue and marsh woundwort. These are vital refuges for small birds such as sedge warblers, reed buntings, wagtail and snipe.

Where the river banks are not cleared of vegetation, they make a rich linear habitat with colourful plants including iris, hemp agrimony, comfrey, purple loosestrife and vetches. The insects supported by these flowers attract swallows and martins. Willows and alders provide seeds for warblers and siskins. Bridge arches and steep banks of gravel pits are used as nest sites for swallows and sand martins respectively.

The river itself supports a variety of fish; found here are roach and bleak, a member of the carp family, as well as gudgeon, perch, dace, bream and several others. These are preyed upon by kingfishers, grebes, swans and herons. Mallard and Canada geese feed on the stems, buds and seeds of water plants, the geese also feeding on land, often spoiling farmers crops.

Dragonflies and damselflies vary in their habitat preferences. Many depend on stagnant water in marshes or shallow pools, others need slow moving rivers and

Siskin on alder

canals or the calmer reaches of otherwise faster flowing
water. The adults and larvae feed on smaller insects such
as mosquitoes, midges, caddis and mayflies. In turn they
are taken by pike and bream, frogs, swallows and herons.
They are thus an essential link in the food chain of
wetlands and their abundance indicates a healthy
freshwater environment. Unfortunately, land drainage
for agriculture and development, coupled with pollution
by effluent and pesticides has drastically reduced their

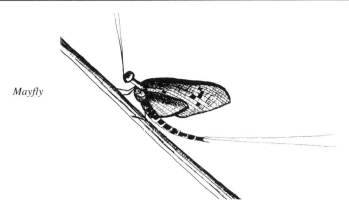

Mayfly

numbers in many locations. Survival of streams in the Thames valley, especially between Sonning and Shiplake, and of water filled clay pits and small ponds on the Chiltern plateau, together with improvement in quality of water and riverbank habitats, will protect these fascinating insect pest controllers.

══	Road
▬ ▬ ▬ ▬	Circular Walk
▬■▬■▬	Walk on road
───	Track
- - - -	Footpath
∿∿∿	Stream or River
⬯	Pond or lake
■	Building
▨	Residential
⌘	Deciduous trees
⋏	Conifers
⌐⌐	Grassland
+	Church
P H	Public House
N T	National Trust
┼┼┼┼┼	Railway line
Spr	Spring
F B	Footbridge
S C	Short cut
A R	Alternative route

Key to individual route maps

23

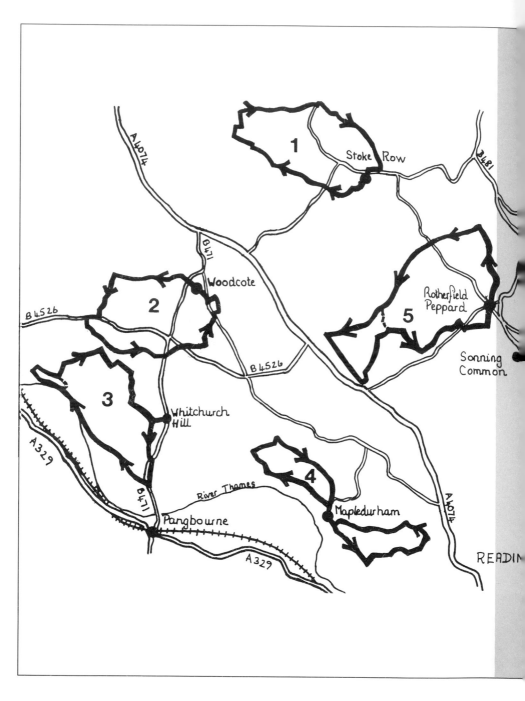

Locations of the Walks

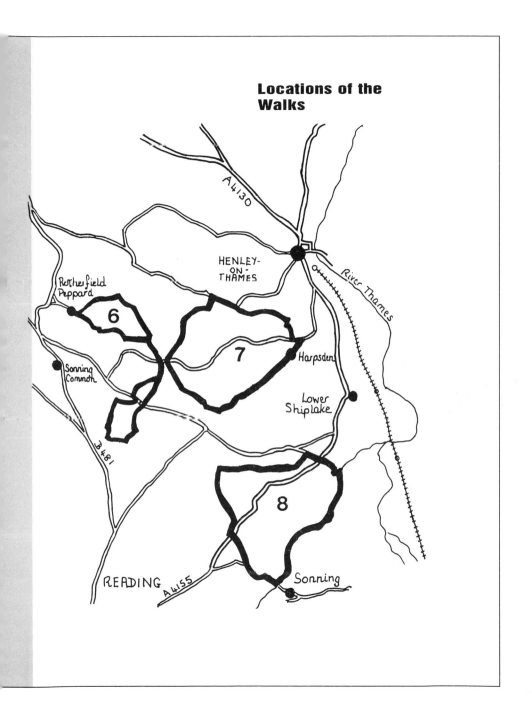

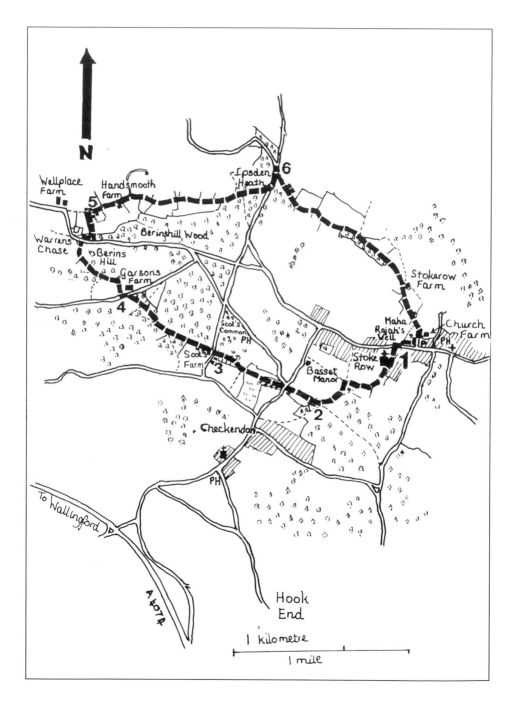

N

Wellplace Farm
Handsmooth Farm
5
Berinshill Wood
Warrens Chase
Berins Hill
Garsons Farm
4
Ipsden Heath
6
Stokerow Farm
Maha Rajah's Well
Church Farm
PH
Scot's Common PH
Stoke Row
1
Scot's Farm
3
Basset Manor
2
Checkendon
PH
To Wallingford
A 4074
Hook End
1 kilometre
1 mile

26

Stoke Row

5.5 miles   9 km

This walk uses many old tracks through quiet woods and fields, some of which will be muddy in wet weather. There are some steep slopes and a good viewpoint over the Chiltern escarpment.

1. SU678840

Start from School Lane beside the parish church and follow the lane 100m past the end of the houses until a path leads off to the right, signed to Checkenden. It leads between fences straight across a field into a woodland strip. Turn left past buildings along the edge of the trees with a fence on the left. Continue downhill in woodland along a fenceline on the right to the bottom of the hill. Here turn right along a track leading out of the woods.

Stoke Row originated as a tiny hamlet bordering a small area of open commonland and the village has grown up since the common was enclosed in the middle of the last century; the parish church of St John the Evangelist was built in 1846. This area was well known as being a centre for bodgers who turned chair parts, often working in the surrounding woods. A few continued in this trade until the 1940's, their workshops based at The Cherry Tree and The Crooked Billet, local pubs in Stoke Row (see Introduction).

As you pass the church, look out for jackdaws, members of the crow family, which live in the tower. These birds are often found in close association with people. Churchyards are often places with nature conservation interest because of infrequent mowing and lack of disturbance. Here look for bluebells and other spring flowers.

As you walk along the lane notice the contrast between the hedges. Those on the right contain many different species and are likely to be the old field hedges. On the left, look for a conifer hedge of cypress trees, a fast growing species now frequently used for hedging. In the 1970's, a small moth normally resident on the continent, called Blair's shoulder knot, which feeds on cypress, managed to settle in England. Since then it has gradually spread northwards across southern England, colonising garden hedges.

When you reach the woodland strip look across the fields to your right and you will be able to see Basset Manor. This has been known as a manor house since 1695 but earlier it was an ordinary farm, although it is alleged to be on the site of a Norman hunting lodge.

This woodland, Ipsden Wood, belongs to the Chiltern Forest, part of the Forestry Commission. Much small beech is present at the top of the slope, probably reflecting past timber extraction. In the valley bottom and beyond, fast growing conifers produce commercial timber for use in paper making and fencing posts. Wood for over 8000 tonnes of newsprint and 4,500km of fencing is produced annually from the Chiltern Forest, a major change from the traditional products, but allowing continuation of managed woodland.

2. SU673835

Follow the track on the right, past a cottage and along a lane to the road. Here cross straight over and take the footpath over a stile beside a gate. Cross the field and follow the path, keeping the wood edge on the left. At a gap at the top left corner of the field, bear left for a short distance but then continue in the same

Cottage on Scot's Common

**direction as before, along a track and over a stile
close to a cottage, through trees until you reach Scot's
Farm.**

As you approach the end of the lane, close to a barn,
notice the hops growing in the hedge on the right. They
have fresh green leaves and clusters of greenish papery
fruits in summer, the leaves becoming yellow and the
fruits brown in autumn. Hops have long been used for
flavouring beer, but were not cultivated until the 16th
century. This particular specimen is growing close to its
unlikely near relatives – stinging nettles and elm.

The landscape in this area is very typical of the
south Chilterns with small fields, interspersed with
woodland and scattered dwellings. The woodland varies
from large blocks like Ipsden Wood to narrow strips or
shaws like those here. Some woodland has developed
on old commonland; the woodland on your right as you
approach Scot's Farm was originally Scot's Common.
If you have an Ordnance Survey 1:25000 map you can
see from place names where else this may have occurred.

29

3. SU662839

At Scot's Farm, cross the road and follow the track opposite past some modern houses. The track leads into woodland, then downhill. In the valley bottom, cross another track and climb the slope opposite. Continue along the path, ignoring forestry tracks, to emerge on the road.

Scot's Farm is an old site as reflected by the huge pollarded oak standing at the gate. Across the track is an overgrown pond which must have been used in the past for water for the farm. Some ponds were drained during the war to avoid the possibility of disease, but many have just gradually fallen into disuse and have become overgrown with vegetation. However it is surprising how even the smallest patch of seasonal water can be an important habitat for wildlife, so that an over-

Oak pollard, Scot's Farm

grown pond may not be the habitat loss it appears to be.

The road which you cross here is part of the ancient Chiltern Ridgeway running along the crest of the hills. It was used as an alternative winter route for the Icknield Way along the foot of the escarpment which became very muddy in wet weather.

In the woodland there are two related plants which are both ferns. Bracken has leaves which arise separately from underground stems or rhizomes (which makes it very difficult to eradicate where it has become a pest). Male fern has leaves or fronds arising in a clump close together. Modern ferns are related to an ancient group of plants and reproduce by brownish spores produced in sacks called sori beneath the leaf surface. This is in marked contrast to later evolved plants such as conifers and flowering plants which have reproductive structures arranged in tight clusters such as in cones or flowers, separating the functions of leaves and reproduction. Fossil evidence has shown that ferns were abundant in the Carboniferous period about 350 million years ago and were a major component of coal which was formed at that time. In contrast flowering plants with their seeds probably did not evolve until the Jurassic period about 150 million years ago.

Look out for the numerous pits and hollows in the woods. The smaller roughly rectangular hollows are old sawpits where timber was cut into planks, although now reduced in size due to erosion of the soil. The larger holes are chalkpits where chalk was dug for putting on the fields to improve the texture of clay soil.

The many beech trees are often found on thin soils whereas oak only grows on deeper moist ground, often on the hill tops. In spring notice the tassels of male beech flowers which later fall off once their pollen has blown away. The female flowers produce the beech mast or nuts. The amount produced varies from year to year but there is often a bumper crop about every four years. The tree does not reproduce north of the Midlands as it needs warm summers to ripen the seed. The nuts are good food for squirrels, chaffinches, blue and great tits, especially in winter.

Great tit (left) and blue tit

4. SU654844

At the road turn left for 50m then right over a stile past Garsons Farm. Follow the path to the side of the farm then into Berins Wood. Bear left on an ill-defined path, through a holly grove, keeping to the edge of the woodland. Look out for the white arrows. After about 200m at a junction follow the path to the right, following arrows again. At the edge of the wood, cross a stile into a field. Continue down to the next stile, then go straight on with the hedge on the right down a track to the road. Cross and take the path opposite along the edge of a hollow way. After about 150m, look out for a path off to the left which leads down to a stile into a field. Keep to the left edge of the field, cross over a fence and go through the gate past some buildings (beware there may be fierce dogs here) to a lane close to Wellplace Farm.

Garsons Farm buildings display a range of ages. The front of the house and other buildings are brick-and-flint or, more recent, brick used alone. The back of the farm is half timbered and probably the oldest part. The building materials would all have been produced locally, the bricks perhaps at Nettlebed or Stoke Row.

Amongst the rubble in the yard at the back of Garsons Farm can be seen Oxford ragwort, a non-native plant with an interesting history. The plant, a native of Sicily, was originally brought to Oxford Botanic gardens in the 18th century, reputedly collected from the slopes of volcanic Mount Etna. Wind-blown seeds colonised the limestone walls of the garden and then spread through the country along the clinker of the 19th century railway track network which resembled its natural dry habitat. Now Oxford ragwort can be found in many dry, stony and built-up places.

The holly in Berins Wood is a common understorey shrub found in this area. It never grows into the typical conical shape of a holly tree in the open. Look at the small yellow-brown blemishes on some of the leaves. These mark the feeding sites of the larvae of a small fly, the holly leaf miner, living inside the leaf. See if you can find any mines with V-shaped tears; these show where blue tits have been feeding on the insects.

Pause to look at the view as you emerge from the wood on Berins Hill. You can see the edge of the Chiltern escarpment, which here is quite shallow compared with the steeper slopes to the north. The Thames valley is spread out to the left with the Berkshire Downs rising on the far side. The massive buildings of Didcot Power Station dominate the view, a marked contrast to the small scale impact of human activity in earlier times. The open landscape of the valley contrasts with the wooded aspect of the hills and reflects the historical differences in land-use (see Introduction). Changes in land use are still happening; a recent development is the use of autumn sown cereals which give the fields a green cover during winter, a contrast to the brown ploughed fields of the recent past.

The hollow way which runs parallel to the lane and the footpath shows the age of this route which is one of several leading from Ipsden in the valley to the commons on the hills. You will be following another such route further on.

Wellplace Farm is so named from the ruined well here, reputedly Roman but actually medieval.

5. SU651852

Turn right along the metalled bridleway to a junction with a track leading to Handsmooth Farm. Continue along the bridleway as it winds up the valley, eventually leading into woods and emerging onto the road. Turn left and continue for about 150m to a junction, to take the bridleway on the right.

Notice the many rooks which can be seen on the slopes of the grazed fields alongside the track. They feed on insects and are useful in breaking up the cowpats as they search for food. It is now recognised that rooks are not such pests as they were previously thought to be. The benefit they give by reducing insect pests compensates for damage to cereal crops.

There are pleasant views to be had down the valley. The mixed hedges and hedgerow flowers in spring and summer, and the varied autumn colours of leaves and fruit add to the enjoyment of the track.

There is evidence of many rabbits here. Their burrows are found in the banks alongside the track, where often elder is the only shrub growing there. Rabbits do not like elder so it is the only shrub which survives. Crush and smell a growing leaf to see why! Originally introduced by the Normans, rabbits were prized for their meat and kept in special manmade warrens. However over the centuries they escaped into the countryside and became pests, damaging crops and young trees. The myxomatosis epidemic in the 1950's reduced the population drastically but now the disease does not have such an effect and the population is increasing again.

Two flowers from the *Umbelliferae* or carrot family can be found here. Along the hedgerow, look for the familiar cow parsley, with finely divided leaves and a spreading loose white flowerhead, while in the woods, sanicle with rounded uncut leaves and small compact pinkish flowerheads, can be seen. This latter plant typically only grows in old woodland on chalky soil so is not widespread throughout the countryside. As well as sanicle look for other indicators of old woodland such as sweet woodruff. Another plant to spot in early spring is snowdrop; it is not known if these have been planted here or are growing wild.

This route was more important in the past as it led to Ipsden Heath, the woods ahead, which, until the mid 19th century, were open heath and wood pasture for grazing and fuel collection. This is still a wooded common where commoners have the right of estover or collection of fallen timber for firewood. As you enter the woodland look for a bank on the right which marks the old boundary of the Heath. The wood is now predominantly mature forest with beech, oak, ash, cherry and whitebeam, a typical Chiltern mix of species. However a proportion of these species were felled in the 1960's and replanted with conifers. The wood now belongs to the Woodland Trust which aims to replace the conifers with broadleaf trees again to conserve the woodland for wildlife and for visitors.

Fairy ring of
toadstools

In autumn, toadstools, one of several types of fungal

35

fruiting bodies may be glimpsed under the trees. You may see rings of brownish toadstools growing beneath the trees. Fungal spores line the fleshy gills beneath the caps and are easily dislodged to disperse and proliferate this more advanced type of fungus. More commonly this group of fungi form 'fairy rings' in grassland. The grass within the ring is often killed when the fungal threads clog up the air spaces in the soil, leading to waterlogging. This phenomenon was attributed to the dancing feet of fairies and elves until the real cause was discovered in the 19th century. Many of the old stumps are covered by the black and white antler-like structures of the candle snuff fungus, so called because of its black stacks and powdery white tips, resembling the burnt wicks of candles. This different type of fungus is representative of flask fungi with spores originating from deep pits beneath the surface of the fruiting body.

The road is another section of the Chiltern Ridgeway, described earlier.

6. SU668857

Taking the bridleway which leads off at the junction to the right, follow it through woodland, then past barns and a house, continuing between hedges and then alongside a woodland strip. Eventually the track becomes a farm road and leads past the entrance to Stoke Row Farm and then Church Farm. Just before reaching the main road, turn right through an old cherry orchard and walk about 100m past the Maharajah's Well back to the starting point.

Along the track look out for signs of old hedge management. There are many trees with massive horizontal stems which have grown since the hedge was last laid, many years ago. Coppiced hazel can also be seen, the new growth used for poles around the farm or garden in the past. The track varies in width; in some places it is a level track, in others a sunken hollow way. This probably reflects differences in the underlying geology or topography.

In the late spring, notice house martins, with con-

House martins collecting mud

spicuous white rumps and blunt forked tails, flying near Stoke Row Farm. They collect mud from puddles and ruts in the track to build their nests on walls just under the eaves of buildings.

The land between Stoke Row Farm and Church Farm is bordered by two types of hedges with different origins and values. To the left is the sinuous line of a very mixed species hedgerow probably a remnant of woodland left after the adjacent fields were formed many centuries ago. The fruits and berries of hazel, holly, dog rose, ash, blackthorn and hawthorn will sustain animals and birds through the winter and the thick prickly shrubs provide nest sites and shelter. In comparison, the pure beech hedge around the garden opposite, although attractive and useful as a boundary and barrier is less likely to attract wildlife seeking food. However, beech, when used as hedging, retains its leaves in winter, so this will provide shelter for birds or small mammals.

Maharajah's Well

The Maharajah's Well is unmistakeable. Built in an oriental style, the well and machinery were installed in 1864 as a gift from the Maharajah of Benares who had been horrified to hear from the District Commissioner, Edward Reade of Ipsden, that this village in England had no water supply. The well was dug to a depth of 365 feet through the chalk until the water table was reached. The land next to the well was planted with cherry trees, the sale of the cherries helping to pay for the upkeep of the well. There are many more details on the information boards at the well.

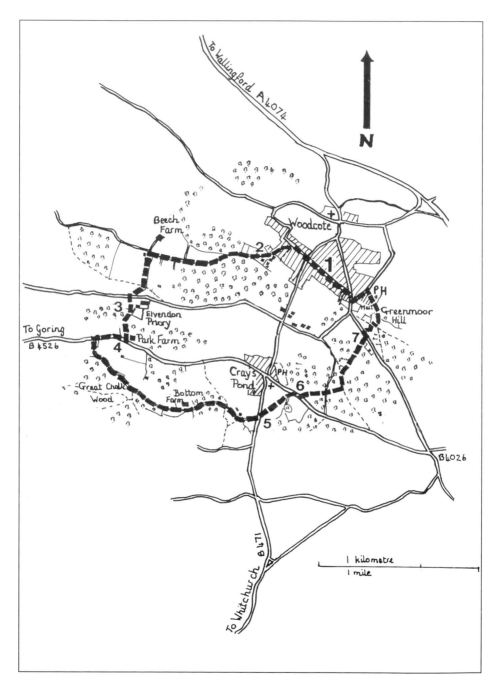

To Wallingford A4074

N

Beech Farm

Woodcote

2

1

PH

Greenmoor Hill

Hall

3

Elvendon Priory

To Goring B4526

Park Farm

4

7

Crays Pond

PH

Great Chalk Wood

Bottom Farm

6

5

B4026

To Whitchurch B471

1 kilometre
1 mile

WALK 2

Woodcote

5.5 miles 9 km

This is a varied walk with some good views across the Thames valley and attractive Chiltern valleys and woods. The going is mostly easy with two short steepish climbs.

1. SU643816

Start from the residential roads Bridlepath or Beech Lane.

At the end of Bridlepath cross the road beside the supermarket and walk along Beech Lane, bearing left at the next junction where the lane becomes narrower. After about 0.5km you will reach open countryside.

Two hundred years ago Woodcote consisted of a scattering of cottages around the edge of a large expanse of rough ground known as Woodcot Common which linked with an even larger tract of open land – Goring Heath, a remnant of which you will see later. Tracks led across the common, one of which was the road you walk along called Bridlepath. The common was enclosed in 1853 by Act of Parliament. Common land was always situated on poor ground, not good for agriculture (see Introduction). Hence, many Chiltern commons were of little use after enclosure and were gradually sold for building land, giving rise to the variation in architectural styles in such villages. Bridlepath and Beech Lane are interesting; they are both roads which existed before enclosure and have developed gradually over the last two hundred years. By noticing the style of the architecture of the houses this evolution can be traced. Look out for Victorian cottages, Edwardian villas, pre-war semi-detached houses or bungalows and 1960's equivalents. Notice also the relationship of the houses with their environment. The older cottages tend to be built of local materials, brick, sometimes with flint, but more modern buildings are made of mass produced materials which can be seen anywhere and which do not have a regional character.

2. SU634818

Follow the quiet road for almost 1km until you reach a track signed to the left, opposite a lane leading to Beech Farm. Follow the track across the field and at a gap in the hedge cross the stile. Cross a bridleway and another stile, taking the path downhill across a field, walking diagonally to the right to a stile beside a telegraph pole.

According to Davis's map of Oxfordshire made in 1797, all the area along Beech Lane was then wooded. The fields on the right are therefore relatively recent additions to the landscape. The hedge on the right of the lane contains many woodland shrubs and trees, including oak, beech, hazel, field maple and dogwood, all of which can be seen in the wood on the left. Therefore this hedge may be a remnant strip of woodland, left behind when clearing took place, or could have been planted along the lane using saplings growing nearby. Notice also the distinct wood bank along the left side of the lane. This may have marked the boundary of a detached part of Dorchester Hundred, an enclave situated within Langtree Hundred which covers the rest of this area. If this is the case, then the bank is at least a thousand years old, and possibly older than that!

In autumn, the lane is spectacular with views of changing leaf colours. Several species can be identified at a distance by their colour and timing of leaf fall. Ash leaves retain their green colour and are drab compared with the bronze of beech, the golden brown of oak and the bright orange red of cherry. The change of colour indicates the efforts of the trees to retain some of their important chemical reserves by breaking down and recycling their green chlorophyll, thus exposing other pigments in the leaf to produce the typical rich autumn colours.

The buildings of Beech Farm date back to the 17th century. It is a typical isolated Chiltern farm, probably dating back to the early Middle Ages when clearings or assarts were made in woodland for agriculture. The farm lane is lined with old cherry trees, once an important fruit crop in the Chilterns. Wild cherry trees can also be seen in the woodland, distinctive with their white spring blossom and coloured autumn leaves.

The landscape is more open as the track leads across the field. You may see or hear an occasional skylark but this once common farmland bird is in sharp decline. The modern practice of ploughing in cereal stubble in early autumn, and sowing winter wheat which is treated with pesticides, removes weed seeds and insect food sources needed by the birds. However set-aside land filled with arable weeds may replace these diminishing food sources.

Skylark

Pheasants are reared in this area and may frequently be seen in the surrounding fields. This bird was introduced to this country around the 11th or 12th century and spread rapidly in England. Systematic gamekeeping of pheasants for sport began in the 18th century. Very harsh penalties for poaching caused tensions between landowners and the ordinary people. However, pheasant rearing now performs a valuable service in retaining wild life habitats in an agricultural landscape. Many field edges and corners are planted with feed crops and cover for game birds, which also benefit other wild birds, rabbits, foxes and deer. Even though such management seems important, more wild than reared pheasants are shot. Look for pheasant foot prints in the muddy patches on the path, along with those of horses, dogs and people.

Pheasant

As you descend the grassy slope, notice a few flowers of white clover, spear thistle, black medick and daisy. This grassland has been "improved" for grazing by the use of artificial fertilisers and pesticides and so is very different to the flower-rich chalk grassland which can be seen later along the walk.

Note the woodland edge at the top right hand corner of this field. The beech trees are tall and thin with most of their branches at the top. Such trees have grown in the shade of others, becoming tall to reach the light high up in the canopy. Some of the sturdier edge trees have either fallen in the gales of the late 1980's or have been felled, so exposing these more vulnerable trees which are likely to be more easily damaged by strong winds.

3. SU623813

Cross the road and take the grassy path opposite uphill alongside a hedge. At the top follow the tarred track uphill through woodland and past Park Farm until you reach the road where you turn right.

The buildings to the left are called Elvendon Priory and, although they are mainly 20th century, they incorporate the remains of a medieval house which may have been a house of retreat for Goring Priory. The name Elvendon means "fairy hill".

In spring the tarred track is lined with planted daffodils but there are other wild spring flowers to be seen such as wood anemones and bugle. In summer rosebay willow herb and bramble flowers are good food sources for bees and other insects. The flowers flourish here as the open woodland allows much light to reach the ground. In thick beech woods the ground is often bare of vegetation, because the dense shade does not allow sufficient light for most plants to grow.

Listen for woodland birds here such as robins, blue and great tits, chaffinches and pheasants. Chiffchaffs are migrants, flying from Africa each spring, arriving in mid March. They have a distinctive song, calling their own name repetitively.

Park Farm has an old flint barn and an old granary raised by staddle stones above ground level to keep rats and damp out of the grain. Nowadays, grain is dried mechanically and stored in controlled conditions. Redundant staddle stones are often seen as garden ornaments.

4. SU623809

Walk with care along the road for about 300m, then take the marked bridleway on the left. At the wood, bear left following blue arrows and walk along the edge of Great Chalk Wood. At a junction again bear left, continuing as before along the edge of the wood.

Carry on through a gate alongside a paddock past Bottom Farm and follow the lane past some cottages until you reach the road.

As you walk along the road there is a fine view of the Goring Gap, where the River Thames flows between the chalk hills of the Chilterns and the Berkshire Downs. The road itself is part of an old pack horse route between Goring and Henley, used to shorten the journey along the Thames. Barges would be unloaded at Goring and reloaded at Henley to miss out the large curve in the river between these towns.

The verge on the right is a good example of grassland which seems to have escaped improvement. You will find yellow vetchling, agrimony, knapweed, field scabious, toadflax and ox-eye daisy during the summer. This verge, together with the adjacent hedge is an important wildlife refuge between the road and agricultural land. Fast-moving traffic produces wind draughts that can stun and injure butterflies and other insects, but these are then food for crows and magpies, in the same way as rooks can often be seen feeding along motorway hard shoulders.

Further on along the bridleway, look for burdock, a

Agrimony

Burdock

Great mullein

stout plant with large leaves resembling rhubarb. In the past the young stems were eaten in salads and used to flavour drinks such as "dandelion and burdock". It produces prickly fruits called burs which hook on to animal fur or human clothing so that the heavy seeds are dispersed over a wide area. The plant has several regional names which reflect the characteristic appearance of the leaves – wild rhubarb and pig's rhubarb – and its seeds – bachelor's buttons.

Another plant to look out for along this part of the path are tall yellow flowered spikes of mullein with soft felty leaves. Great Mullein or Aaron's rod, referring to the biblical description, contains soapy chemicals that form a lather when mixed with water; this has been used to treat lung disease in humans and cattle. The name mullein may be a corruption of the Old English word *wulleyn* meaning woollen, referring to the texture of the leaves.

Great Chalk Wood seems to have had a varied past with parts being planted since the early 1800's. There is evidence of coppicing in some places with large stumps (stools) of hazel. In other areas, woodlands shown as coniferous on the modern Ordnance Survey map, are now filled with ash and willow and the conifers have gone. Both ash and willow can colonise open ground successfully, their seeds spread easily by the wind.

As you walk along the valley bottom, notice the ivy covering many of the tree trunks. The flowers in autumn are a valuable late food source for bees, wasps, and flies, which are often so numerous on sunny days that their buzzing can be heard from quite a distance.

In the grassy paddocks close to Bottom Farm, on bright moist autumn or winter days, look out for the carpets of spiders silk covering the vegetation. Small spiders often spin long silk threads which they let blow in the breeze, then use as parachutes to help carry them to new areas. Spider silk is famed for its strength and other properties. Scientists are researching its chemical make-up so that it can be artificially produced for numerous uses.

Bottom Farm and the cottages nearby are shown on

Bluebells

the Oxfordshire map of 1797, the cottages then bordering the large open area of Goring Heath.

Past Bottom Farm the path is bordered by wild flowers, many of which are indicators of old woodland. Wood spurge, wood mellick, wood sorrel and wood ruff are all examples; bluebells, primroses, violets and foxgloves all add colour. The plentiful fallen wood is a good site for numerous fungi, mainly conspicuous in autumn.

5. SP636802

At the road, turn left and cross with care.

EITHER – take the path diagonally across the grass. At the road, cross, turn right and walk for 100m to a path leading left into the woods (rejoining the guide at Point 6)

OR – walk along the grass parallel to the road to Cray's Pond. At the junction, turn right and continue for 350m until a footpath leads off to the left into woodland.

The open grass is a remnant of the vegetation of Goring Heath, a large area of commonland stretching from here, south to Whitchurch Hill and east to present day Goring Heath. To the north it linked with Woodcote Common. The Heath was enclosed in 1806, making way for an ordered landscape of fields and straight roads.

A plant to look out for in the grass is hairy tare, with white flowers, a member of the vetch family. It was a troublesome cornfield weed due to its trailing stems which earned it the nickname of strangle tare.

The pond at the corner was originally called Gray's Pond and is likely to be an old one as it was listed in the Enclosure Act. It is attractive with wet loving plants like reed mace and large sedges growing in the water while yellow iris or flag grows on the banks. If you pause to rest on the seat look out for dragon flies, a common sight in summer. The males set up territories to court females and chase away other males.

The tree shading the bench is an ornamental crab apple, Golden Hornet, a variety of a Japanese species, with small yellow fruits in autumn. You may have noticed other crab apples along the route. The true crab has spines on the twigs and the apples are usually small and green. Other apples you may see have sprung from domesticated apple trees and are various colours and shapes.

Hairy tare

49

6. SP640804

**Follow the path into woods, following the most
obvious route. When you reach a wide muddy track
turn right for 10m then left into the woods, following
the white arrows on the trees. The paths are quite
hard to follow in this wood so concentrate on the
route! The path leads over a bank and then continues
for 150m to a junction marked by arrows. Turn left
here for 100m, then right at the next junction. The
path passes a rectangular earthwork and carries
straight on to reach a road.**

The first section of woodland has probably grown up
since the enclosure of Goring Heath, although there were
always patches of woodland here. The linear banks mark
old boundaries between common and woodland, but the
purpose of the possibly pre-medieval rectangular
earthwork is not known. Notice how the woodland is
different on each side of some banks,reflecting different
management in each section. Young woodland
containing a mixture of beech, cherry and birch changes
to older woodland of holly and mature beech all of a
similar size, indicating that it was planted at the same
time.

Notice how moss grows on the banks but not on the
ground. This may be because the fallen leaves blow off
the banks and so do not shade out the plants from light
or moisture.

7. SP647809

**The path emerges on to the road opposite an old
chapel, now a house. Turn left uphill for 100m then
take the bridleway to the right and follow it parallel
to the garden fence to reach a track. Here turn right,
then soon left up an old track to the Black Lion public
house. Turn left along the road for 400m going past
the radio mast. At the junction turn right, then left
to the starting point in either Bridlepath or Beech
Lane.**

The Methodist church dates from 1886 and is a typical

Victorian brick building, contrasting with the older brick and flint cottages seen elsewhere.

The old cottages here again date back to the days before Woodcote Common was enclosed, making it obvious that most of present day Woodcote is a relatively modern settlement. Along the track, at the entrance to Greenmoor Hill, look back for a good view over the nearby woods to the Berkshire hills beyond Reading.

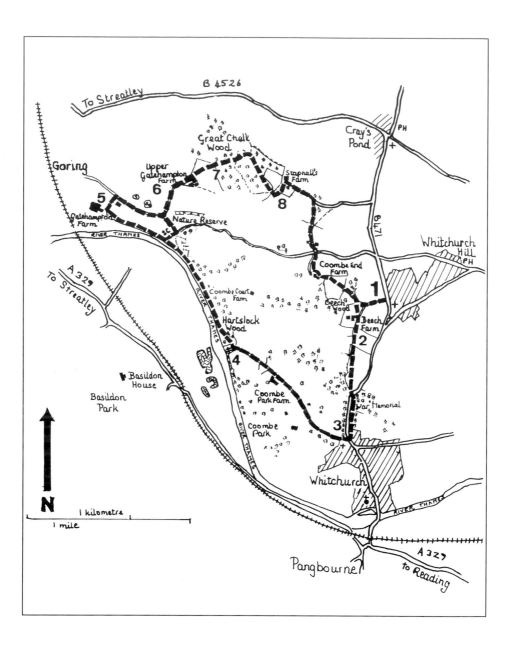

To Streatley   B 4526

Cray's Pond   PH

Goring

Great Chalk Wood

Upper Gatehampton Farm   6

5

Gatehampton Farm

RIVER THAMES

Nature Reserve

Stapnall's Farm

7

8

Whitchurch Hill   PH

A 329

To Streatley

Coombe Court Farm

RIVER THAMES

Coombe End Farm

1

Beech Wood

Beech Farm

2

Hartslock Wood

4

Basildon House

Basildon Park

Coombe Park Farm

Coombe Park

War Memorial

3

Whitchurch

RIVER THAMES

N

1 kilometre

1 mile

Pangbourne

A 327

to Reading

Whitchurch

6 miles   10 km

Short cut 5.5 miles   9 km

This route passes through a scenic stretch of the Thames valley and then climbs through fields and woodland along mostly good paths

1. SU637789

Start close to St John the Baptist church at Whitchurch Hill on the B471 and take the concrete track opposite. At Beech Farm go straight on into the field, through the metal kissing gate, turning left at the wire fence. Cross the drive in front of the house, continue along a wooden fence and through another kissing gate on to a grassy track.

The regular passage of vehicles along the track influences the pattern of encroaching vegetation. Vigourous plant growth occurs only in the centre of the track and the edges. This effect can be seen in many fields with the obvious bare paths where sheep walk in line and around field gates where animals often congregate. In all these places, a special collection of plants are found which are low growing, flat or creeping types, or else, like grass have their growing centres close to the ground. Tall plants which grow from the top are easily damaged and killed.

The hedge has a great variety of different species, producing a profusion of flowers here in the spring. The resulting fruit crop of sloes, hawthorn berries and rosehips are welcome food for birds in winter. Notice that the plants flower and fruit at differing times so that insects, birds and mammals, such as mice and foxes, can usually find food somewhere. The broad swathe of brambles is particularly welcome with flowers and fruit in late summer and autumn. In the hedge bottom, notice two closely related members of the bedstraw family. On the right is hedge bedstraw with bright white flowers, while the left-hand hedge contains goose grass or cleavers, with paler white flowers. The former is a slender trailing perennial plant but cleavers is a pernicious annual weed, its fruits, stems and leaves clinging tenaciously by small prickles to animal fur and human clothing, thus dispersing its seeds.

Beech Farm is a typical example of the use of local building materials which reflect the underlying geology. The red bricks and tiles may have been made locally in the south Chilterns and, together with the knapped flints in the garden wall, indicate the clay-with-flints deposits which overlie much of the chalk hills of the Chilterns.

2. SU634786

The grassy path leads to another kissing gate; carry on along the field edge with woodland on the right. At the far end of the field another kissing gate leads downhill through woodland to the road. At the road turn right, continuing past the war memorial. Cross to walk along the path bordering the road. Turn right just before the bottom of the hill along the bridleway signed to Goring.

(Carry on into Whitchurch to see the river, lock and weir. Return to this point to continue).

Along the grassy path there are good views to the right down a steep valley which is called Coombe Bottom on a map dating from 1761. There are several farms and houses here which include Coombe in their names. This word comes from an Anglo-Saxon word *cumb* which described a short broad valley. Later in the walk you will pass across the base of this valley.

As you walk through this peaceful rural landscape,

the late 20th century intrudes with the sound of traffic on the nearby road. Nowadays there are few places where traffic noise is not heard; luckily many Chiltern valleys tend to be quiet.

Notice the thicket of snowberry on the right over the fence. This shrub was introduced from North America in the early 19th century and is sometimes planted for pheasant cover. The white berries stay on the bushes all winter and in the numbers seen here are an attractive contrast to the more common red berries of native plants like hawthorn and holly.

As you walk through the woodland towards the road, in summer look for one of the commoner orchids to be found in Chiltern woodlands, the self descriptive broad-leaved helleborine. Most unusually for woodland plants, their dull pinkish flowers appear in late summer.

3. SU633776

Follow the bridleway for about 1.5km (1 mile), going straight on at a junction of tracks. At a bend to the left, take the path to the right, down some steps. The path crosses a valley then climbs steeply to enter woodland.

The bridleway passes beside the old park land belonging to Coombe Lodge. A mansion was built here in the late 18th century, described fifty years later as "a majestic building". Now only the kitchen remains. The past splendour of Coombe Park can be glimpsed with specimen trees and grass sweeping down to the river to the left. Many of the trees have low spreading branches and were probably pollarded in the past which encouraged this shape.

Along the track look out for a line of elms, a variety resistant to Dutch Elm disease. Unlike the English elm they are not susceptible to the fungus-carrying Scolytus beetle which bores into the bark. Notice how in winter the arrangement of young branches resemble a cartoon fish back bone! There are some English elm saplings nearby in the hedge, but they are likely to succumb to the disease after a few more years.

The valley crossed by the path is the one which you looked down earlier. From here you can see that it is indeed short and broad!

4. SU622784

The path enters Hartslock Wood and continues gradually descending to river level. It continues parallel to the river for about1.5km or 1 mile. (As you reach the end of the wood a path climbs to the right into Hartslock Nature Reserve which is well worth a detour).

SHORT CUT Walk through the Nature Reserve over the brow of the hill down to a gate leading on to a track. Turn left along the track until you meet a lane going right uphill to Upper Gatehampton Farm. Here rejoin the main route towards the end of Point 5.

For the full route, continue along the river path until you reach a small group of buildings and a junction of paths.

Hartslock Wood used to be called Harts Wood; there was an old lock on the Thames here in the past, marked as Hart's Old Lock on the 1st Edition Ordnance Survey map published in 1830. Its proximity to the river and sheltered aspect means that the wood has a damper atmosphere than others you are likely to see and so has a different "feel" to the usual Chiltern wood.

In winter when the trees are bare, notice the carpets of moss covering the ground and fallen trees. These delicate plants are very dependent on water to keep active and absorb it over their whole surface as they do not have substantial root systems or internal conducting tissues. Hence they are found in damp shady places where they will not dry out too much.

Early in the year, the hazel catkins mark the advance of spring. Much unseen activity goes on at this time of year and even the catkins are home to a tiny wasp whose larvae feed there. Look for catkins with brown,

Butcher's broom

dead looking tips containing the larvae which will pupate in the soil to produce the adult wasp.

There are many interesting plants to spot in this wood. Butcher's broom, with dark green spiny "leaves", was used in the past for scouring wooden chopping blocks. The spiny leaves are actually flattened stems and often bear a small white flower or a red berry. Teasel is another plant with a practical past use. The prickly mauve flower heads were used by fullers to raise the nap on woven cloth and were widely grown for this purpose. Two other plants have a medicinal use. In late summer the bell-shaped flowers of deadly nightshade are followed by the glossy purple cherry-sized berries which are extremely poisonous. The drug atropine is derived from this plant, used to dilate pupils for eye examinations. Greater celandine, with yellow flowers and a member of the poppy family, is another poisonous plant. Orange latex oozes from the stem if broken, which was used to cure warts and corns. Its use as a medicinal plant means that it is often found in old gardens.

Along the path where the edge has collapsed, notice the great depth of chalk exposed here (see Introduction). The river has cut a channel through the chalk, separating

Greater celandine

Deadly nightshade

the Chilterns from the Berkshire Downs. The river makes large meanders along this valley and the flat flood plain on the opposite side of the river has been gradually formed from deposits left as the river curves under the chalk escarpment.

Where the trees are more open, there is a view across the river of Basildon House which was built of pale yellow Bath stone in 1776 for Sir Francis Sykes. It is now owned by the National Trust.

By the river bank look out for a concrete pillbox, part of a chain of World War II defences which was built along the length of the river to hinder a German advance in the event of invasion. Hartslock Nature Reserve is owned by the Berkshire, Buckinghamshire and Oxfordshire Naturalists' Trust (BBONT). It is an important site nationally with a Site of Special Scientific Interest (SSSI) designation. It is noted for its rich variety of chalk grassland flowers and grasses, unspoilt by fertilizers or pesticides. The chalkhill blue butterfly may be seen flying here in July and August. Its caterpillars

Wartime defensive pillbox

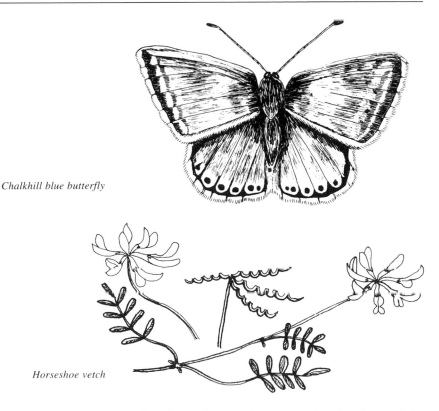

Chalkhill blue butterfly

Horseshoe vetch

feed on horseshoe vetch, named after the shape of the segments of its seed pods.

A guide to the River Thames for "the Tourist, the Oarsman and the Angler" was published in 1872, written and illustrated by Henry Taunt, a well-known Oxford photographer. He describes the flora of this particular part of the Thames valley as being varied and certainly the grassland and the wood still match this description.

If you look back at the reserve you can distinguish it from the other fields; its brownish green is characteristic of old pasture compared with the brighter green of improved grassland.

5. SU609798

When you reach the junction of paths close to the buildings, take the right turn up a rough tarmac

track, alongside a flint wall of Gattendon Lodge. At the top turn right along a narrow lane. When you reach a junction with a bridleway, bear left uphill towards Upper Gatehampton Farm.
(The SHORT CUT rejoins here).

The small group of buildings is all that remains of Gatehampton which in the time of the Domesday Book in 1086 was a village with at least sixteen families split between two manors. Both were held by important Normans and before the Norman invasion had been held by Wigot of Wallingford, a kinsman of King Edward. Later there was a fulling mill and a fishery here but the village was depopulated in 1515 when fourteen people were evicted. The red brick farm was built in the 17th century with later additions. This area has a long history of habitation with a possible Romano British farmstead nearby and a Bronze Age cemetery across the river. The river valley has allowed the development of transport systems, first by water, then road and, later, railway. In turn these have encouraged settlements and their expansion.

6. SU616800

Just before a house towards the top of the hill, take the footpath to the left over a stile. Bear right to a stile beside the stable and over the next field to a stile in the corner. The path leads between two fences to another stile. Continue along the track in the same direction to the near corner of the buildings. The path goes diagonally across the field to a stile into the wood (following roughly the same direction as before).

There are wide views left from this path across to the Berkshire Downs on the far side of the Thames valley above the Goring Gap.

Along the field path you may see several plants which are termed "weeds of cultivation", growing in soil which is regularly disturbed by agriculture. Fat hen, with grey-green leaves, belongs to the "goosefoot" family with leaves said to resemble a bird's foot. The name seems to stem from a belief that it was good for fattening poultry or from its frequent appearance in chicken runs. It was a human food plant for many centuries, the leaves cooked like spinach, and the seeds with a high fat content mixed with other grain. It fell out of use when spinach was introduced in the 19th century. Alternative names of wild pottage and wild spinach reflect this old use. Another plant to look for has blue-white flowers followed by hard grey-brown seeds. This is corn gromwell, with a botanical name *lithospermum* meaning stone seed.

7. SU621803

The path leads into Great Chalk Wood. Follow the obvious narrow grassy path downhill for 100m. Cross a woodland track and at the next junction turn right, then right again at the blue bridleway sign, going uphill.

Entering the wood, there are patches of tall rushy plants to be seen here. This is great wood-rush and can be distinguished by the long white hairs fringing the grasslike leaves. Wood-rush tends to grow in drier places than other rushes and is usually to be found under trees as here.

Wood-rush

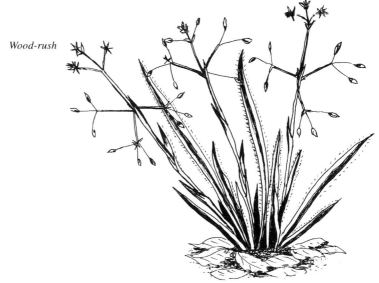

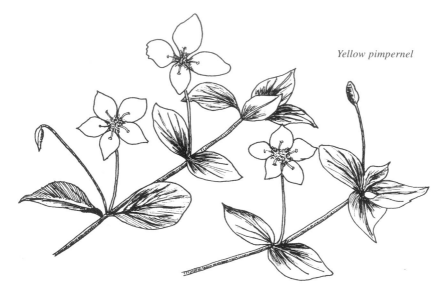

Yellow pimpernel

In spring the woodland is filled with an attractive display of white and blue flowers. White wood sorrel and later sweet woodruff mingle with bluebells and bugle with darker flowers. In June yellow pimpernel can be seen, a relative of the primrose. It looks similar to creeping jenny, another close relative, but can be identified by its more pointed leaves and long flower stalks (see Walk 4 Mapledurham).

The wood here contains many planted conifers which grow faster and so generate a cash crop quicker than hardwoods from deciduous, broadleaved trees. However there is much controversy as to their effect on native insects, birds and plants, which have evolved to live amongst deciduous trees. Where these conifers grow naturally in Europe or North America, the forests are rich in wildlife. Conifers also have an adverse effect by acidifying soils, hence the strong feelings about their cultivation on good soils in southern or lowland areas.

Along the bridleway notice the bank on the left of the path. This probably marked the wood boundary or the roadside as this bridleway was once a more important route. It now marks the boundary between Goring and Goring Heath parishes.

8. SU626799

When you reach a T-junction at the top of the wood go left, soon passing a house. Just past this, turn right through the metal gate then left along the field parallel with the drive. Through a metal five-barred gate turn right along the road. At the junction turn right along the track, passing woodland and, further on, two cottages. Cross the road and continue along the track. At a Y-junction take the left turn then look for a footpath sign opposite a barn. Walk along the field edge with buildings on your right. Cross the stile in the hedge on the right, then make for the stile diagonally left in the fence. Continue in the same direction to a stile at the edge of the woods. The path leads straight on through Beech Wood to emerge at a kissing gate close to Beech Farm. Here retrace your steps left back along the concrete drive to the starting point.

Notice the change in the landscape to the left as you walk along the track and across the fields before entering Beech Wood. It is rather different from the sunken lanes and intimate landscape seen so far today. Here the topography is more level and the aspect open, with oak dominating. In the past this was the edge of Goring Heath, situated on poor sand or gravel soil and uncultivated until the early 19th century when it was enclosed. Notice the hawthorn hedges dividing the fields; these were planted when the heath was enclosed and differ markedly from the older mixed hedges seen earlier along the walk. In Beech Wood, which may have been planted after enclosure, notice the pebbly soil, typical of old common land in this area.

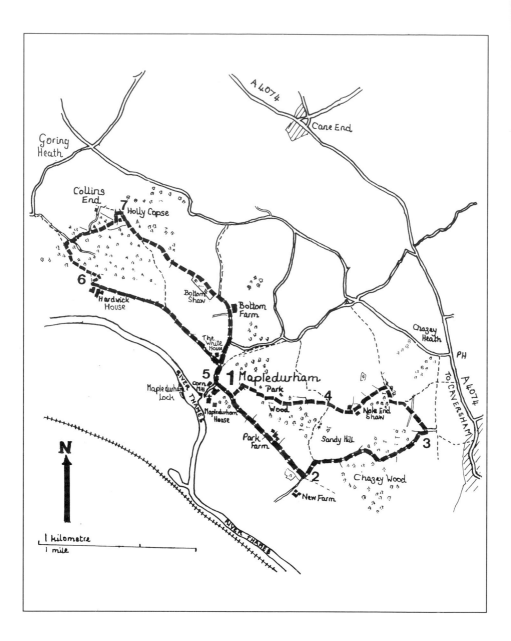

Mapledurham

7 miles 11 km

or two shorter walks each 3.5 miles 6 km

This walk follows a figure of eight so can easily be shortened. Both sections follow the River Thames before climbing gently uphill away from the river and into the hills. Parking in Mapledurham village is quite restricted, with a small car park at the church or a larger one open at weekends between 12.30pm and 5.00pm.

1. SU671768

Mapledurham village is worth a short detour before starting the walk. St Margaret's Church, the water mill and the cottages, particularly the almshouses are worth seeing.

This area has evidence of human activity for many thousands of years, with traces of occupation from about 100 thousand years ago by "Acheulian" man, pre Neanderthal man, who lived during one of the interglacial periods before the last ice age. There is also evidence of Neolithic, Bronze Age and Roman presence here. Mapledurham originally consisted of two manors, Gurny and Chazey with two different entries in the Domesday Book. They were not united until 1582 by Sir Michael Blount who also built the present house in about 1588. The almshouses were founded in 1613, the money coming from the sale of a lease of land at Coxwell in Berkshire (see Book 4). The water mill is

Mapledurham watermill

documented from 1086 onwards when it was worth 20 shillings; it was (and still is) used for grinding corn.

Start the walk at the top of the village, taking the bridleway sign posted to Caversham opposite The Mill House. Continue along this past Park Farm until you reach a junction after about 1.5 km (one mile).

On the right is the River Thames, bordered by flat fields, while the land slopes up to the left. Mapledurham House is on the right and a good view can be had from this path. This Elizabethan mansion replaced a 15th century timber framed house and is a very good example of brickwork of that period, using blue bricks to make a diamond or diaper pattern on the lighter red bricks. In the Civil War the house was fortified by the Royalists but was sacked by the Roundheads during the siege of Reading in 1643.

The track itself is an old one but instead of evolving through use as most paths and bridleways do, this one was made around 1600 by Richard Blount who thus linked Mapledurham with Reading.

As you walk along the track notice the managed landscape here with large fields intensively farmed for high yielding grass crops and grazing. The occasional substantial trees are reminders of the more stately landscape of the past; several are decorative species, grown for leaf colour and tree form. Robinia, false acacia has clumps of mistletoe growing near the top, the seeds spread by birds wiping sticky berries on the branches. Walnut trees are also to be seen with ribbed grey bark. These mature specimen trees contrast with the restricted growth of those seen in crowded woodland conditions.

Further along the bridleway you will reach Park Farm. This was probably the farm which belonged to the manor of Mapledurham Gurny. The present buildings are 17th and 18th century but parts are probably older than this, whilst others are obviously very modern. The large barn was used for threshing corn during the winter months. There are ponds beside the farm and also further

Park Farm

along at New Farm. Most farms had ponds until the 1940's, when many were filled in to prevent spread of disease in farm animals or became silted up. Ponds were important features as they were the only water supply for animals and often for people as well, before the advent of mains supplies, although here the proximity of the river meant that they were perhaps not quite so vital.

2. SU680759

At the junction of tracks, turn left then soon right, past the grain store, and continue uphill into woodland. Once past the trees on the left, in the open again look for a footpath to the left over a stile.

Although much of this land is farmed quite intensively, the borders of the track provide a habitat for wild flowers. In mid summer the bright flowers of yellow sow thistles, pink mallow and red poppies can be found. When the poppy petals fall, they reveal a "pepper pot" shaped fruit capsule which contains the seeds. When they are ripe, the tiny seeds are shaken through a row of small holes under the lid of the pepper pot by a strong breeze and so dispersed.

Further along the track close to the edge of the wood, look for the small bright blue flowers of milkwort, so

Common poppy

68

Milkwort

Black horehound

called because of the belief that animals who grazed on it would produce much milk. It was also thought to be good for nursing mothers. The pink flowers of black horehound can be seen further on to the left. This plant is commonly found on uncultivated woodland edges as here or in hedgerows. An extract of the leaves soaked in water was used in the past as an insect repellent.

As you approach the woodland on the right, look for the bank marking the boundary between the fields and the wood. This is likely to be very old and its presence helped to maintain the shape of the wood for several centuries. Banks also marked ownership or parcels of land used for different purposes. The wood is now sometimes used for paint-ball games, reflecting a new diversification of land use from agriculture to recreation.

As you walk alongside the wood, look left across the valley to the slope opposite. This is Sandy Hill and the land was once part of the fields farmed in common. Prior to its enclosure in 1730, it was opened for cattle grazing by 8th September each year, after the harvest, to graze the weeds and stubble and at the same time to manure the ground. Traces of a trackway and field system on the slope have been seen on aerial photographs.

All this area was known as Mapledurham Chase at the end of the 18th century. This usually refers to a hunting ground but may be a corruption of Chazey, the smaller Mapledurham manor which was situated in this area. The wood is called Chazey Wood as is a farm close to the river south of here.

3. SU693764

The path crosses diagonally left across the field to a stile in a fence. Over the stile follow the path down and uphill, bearing left towards a small wood. Over a third stile, turn right and follow the edge of the wood, keeping the trees on the left. The path rounds the top of the wood and bears left to join a grassy track. Follow this, still with the trees on your left, walking past farm buildings until you reach a concrete path. Continue to a junction.

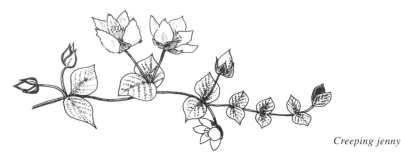

Creeping jenny

The path leads through a field which at the time of writing was uncultivated. The soil here is thin and sandy with numerous stones. It is very dry in summer and difficult to cultivate easily. There are many summer flowering plants here, one of which is dark mullein with yellow petals and purple stamens. It is related to great mullein, a larger plant which can also be seen in dry uncultivated places. The variety of flowers attract many insects; the most obvious are butterflies, particularly common blues and meadow browns. In turn, the seed heads are food for flocks of finches in autumn. These flower-rich uncultivated fields are a marked contrast to those passed at Mapledurham or ahead of you.

On the edge of the small woodland, Noke End Shaw, you can find a plant with yellow flowers, resembling yellow pimpernel (see Walk 3). This is creeping jenny which as its name implies is a prostrate, spreading plant. It has more rounded leaves than yellow pimpernel and shorter, stouter flower stems.

The ground can be quite damp underfoot here, even in the driest weather, as the soil has changed from the sandy, stony ground to thick clay with poor drainage. There is also a small spring here. Making the most of these damp conditions, you can find clumps of rushes growing in the grass and under the trees.

A bird that you may hear or see in this area is the yellowhammer, a sparrow sized bird with a yellow head and chestnut brown body. Its call is easy to identify as it is supposed to say " A little bit of bread and no cheese". Like many other farmland birds, its numbers are declining as it relies mainly on cereal seeds from the

Yellowhammer

stubble and weed seeds in uncut field edges. Stubble is now ploughed in very soon after harvest and fields are often cultivated right up to the margins, leaving no winter store of food for these all year resident birds.

The old farm was formerly called Noke End, End being a very typical Chiltern name for a small hamlet far from the main settlement. These "ends" reflect the late clearing of woodland in the 13th century as agriculture expanded. The old granary is raised on staddle stones to prevent rats and mice climbing up to eat the grain.

4 SU682767

At the junction of tracks take the foot path diagonally left across a field towards trees. Then follow a track through the woods, taking a path which curves off the track downhill to the left. The path emerges from scrub at the bottom of the hill, over a stile, and leads across a grass field back to a stile on the bridleway walked along at the start of the walk. Turn right, back to Mapledurham.

As you stand at the junction, on a clear day notice the landscape around you. To the left of the path is the Thames valley which divides the chalk Downs from the Chilterns. To the right is the Chiltern plateau; it appears to be fairly level but in reality is dissected by many valleys which are hidden from view. The plateau top is mostly tree covered, mainly beech, for which, over many centuries, the Chilterns have been famed. Both Samuel Pepys and Daniel Defoe, in the 17th and 18th centuries respectively, commented on the abundance of beech and its use for firewood. Mapledurham was one of the places on the Thames where beech wood was taken by river to London for fuel. Records of a trader from Wallingford show that wood was sent from here to Queen Elizabeth I around 1570. Several tracks leave this junction but in the past there was another nearby which has now disappeared. On 18th century maps this was called Broad Street and there is evidence of a prehistoric or Roman trackway near by. It is likely that these two routes were the same as "Street" is a common name for routes of Roman origin.

As you cross the field, notice the smooth pebbles in the soil, quite different to the sharp edged flints more usually found in the Chilterns. This smooth shape indicates that they have been deposited by water in the distant past, by a river which followed the approximate line of the Thames.

In the woodland, yellow ragwort grows in open glades. This is the food plant for the caterpillars of the cinnabar moth. They are striped a striking black and yellow; the adult moths are an equally bright crimson and black colour, named after the reddish cinnabar ore from which mercury is extracted. These bright colours are warnings to birds and other animals that these insects are poisonous and unpleasant to eat, having extracted toxins from their ragwort food plant.

Many jays inhabit this woodland. The most colourful member of the Crow family with distinctive blue and white wing patches, it draws attention to itself with strident screeches. Acorns are a favourite food and are carried off and buried. Those not recovered are likely to sprout and thus oak trees colonise neighbouring woodland areas.

The mixture of trees here results in a splendid array of autumn colours, with bright yellow maple and larch,

Jay

orange-red of cherry and the dark green evergreen conifers. Black spots on sycamore leaves in autumn are tar spot fungus, which can reduce tree growth if heavily infected.

As the path descends the slope, notice how the soil changes again, this time to chalk, the underlying strata of the Chilterns, covered in places, as you have seen, with deposits of clay or sandy gravels.

This wood, covering the slope above Mapledurham House, is called Park Wood and is possibly linked to the medieval deer park which was situated in the manor. In 1233 Henry III granted two bucks and ten does from Windsor Forest to Hugh de Gurny for his park here. The park is shown on maps of 1574 and 1603 but no later, so probably made way for agriculture and for landscaped grounds laid out in 1740 by William Kent and Alexander Pope, who was a frequent visitor to the house. A ha-ha was built to divide the former deer park from the gardens. In the woods a folly can be found hidden in the undergrowth, probably placed there when the grounds were landscaped.

5. SU671769

At the end of the bridle way, turn right along the road past the large carpark entrance to a track which leads off to the left beside The White House. Follow this track for 1.5 km (almost a mile), passing through a gateway near a house on the right along the way. At a junction of paths close to Hardwick House turn right uphill.

The White House was formerly an alehouse with a licence to sell snuff. It was called the King's Head in 1841 and many clay pipes for smoking tobacco have been found in the garden. The track from Mapledurham to Whitchurch is an ancient one which was subject to a dispute in 1479. There was an inquisition or enquiry, headed by the then eight year old Prince of Wales, later Edward V, one of the murdered Princes in the Tower of London. Twelve jurors decided that it was a lawful road for use by riders and pack horses.

The verges on both sides are full of interesting flowers, some more common than others. There are two with lilac coloured petals. Vervain has spikes of small flowers and has long been used to treat depression and other nervous disorders. Pale toadflax is like a small snapdragon but with a long spur at the back of the flower. It is an uncommon relative of the widespread garden escape purple toadflax which has much darker flowers on a larger plant. Spindle bushes produce pale green flowers in spring and bright pink seed cases in autumn which split to reveal brilliant orange seeds, sometimes eaten by robins. The stems are hard and smooth and the wood does not splinter so was ideal for making spindles for hand spinning, hence its name.

Rabbits burrow in the banks along the track and their nibbling helps to maintain the flower rich mixture found here by reducing the competition from vigourous grasses for light and nutrients.

To the left there are views of the river and you can get a glimpse of Mapledurham Lock.

At the end of this track you will reach Hardwick House, another old brick building which predates

Pale toadflax

Mapledurham by about 60 years. It was built on a site dating back to the 11th century, owned by the Hardwick family until it was sold to Richard Lybbe who built the house in 1526 and whose family owned it until the 20th century.

6. SU658778

Turn right and follow the path as it bears right uphill past a chalky bank. At the top of the steep slope at a junction take the central path, with a bank to the left and follow the arrows. Continue along the track bearing left at the top of the hill. After 150m there is a turning to the right marked by an arrow. Follow this path downhill; at the bottom turn right opposite a field gate, and then uphill again following the arrows. At the end of the wood, turn left over a stile and out on to a field. Continue up the field with the hedge on your right to a gate.

The exposed white chalk shows clear bands of dark flints, which are formed from silica contained in the chalk. Notice also the thin layer of dark soil on top of the chalk. This is a typical soil over chalk, with just a layer of humus, formed from decayed leaves, without any subsoil between it and the rock beneath.

As you walk uphill there are good views of the river valley over towards the hills beyond Pangbourne. Just before you turn into the wood, the verge on the left contains two attractive groups of plants belonging to the Borage family, both with clusters of funnel shaped flowers. Hound's tongue has maroon flowers and the flattened fruits are covered with short hooked spines which stick to animal fur and human clothing ensuring good seed dispersal. The

Hound's tongue

Comfrey

white or mauve comfrey is renowned for its medicinal use as an ointment to reduce bruising and to heal fractures, hence its traditional names of bruisewort and knitbane.

As you turn into the wood, on the left of the track, beyond the bank, there is a large circular hollow, possibly orginally a quarry, lined with flint and brick walls with broken arches. The structure in the corner of the hollow is "The Sounding House", thought to have been an ice house built of chalk blocks in the 18th century to store ice for use in the summer months.

Running alongside the left side of the track here is a bank which was probably a boundary for woodland management in the past.

7. SU661786

Over the stile (or through the gate), turn right down a tarred bridleway, then between Holly Copse Cottage and a hedge, into woodland. At the junction, marked by an arrow, bear left following the arrows.

Continue walking through woodland, through a gate at the end and on to a chalky track past a woodland strip and Bottom Farm. When you reach the road, turn right and return to Mapledurham.

Holly Copse Cottage is one of several scattered cottages called Collins End, another of the many "ends" in the area as described earlier. The hamlet probably developed at the edge of Goring Heath; a little further north there is still an area called Collinsend Common. If you have an OS map, see how many more "ends" you can find nearby! The track here is a sunken holloway. It is an old route and the passage of feet and time have helped erode away the soil so that it is now below the surrounding land.

The narrow strip of woodland is called Bottom Shaw. "Shaw" is the name given to small patches of woodland and is another frequent landscape description in the Chilterns.

This grassy valley demonstrates another typical landscape feature of the Chilterns. The slope to the left is steeper than that on the right, so that the valley is asymmetrical. It is thought that this landform developed during the ice age when the Chilterns were in the grip of permafrost. The left slope, which faces south-west and is warmed during the day, would have eroded more due to repeated thawing and freezing action than the north-facing slopes which remained frozen.

Bottom Farm has a Victorian farmhouse but an older house was opposite which was probably built in the 17th century. Maps made in the 1700's show several buildings and orchards here. The granary is likely to be a century older than this.

The open fields here are regularly used by rooks to search for insects. They perform a valuable function in keeping down grassland pests such as "leather jackets", the young stages of crane flies, better known as "daddy-long-legs", seen in late summer.

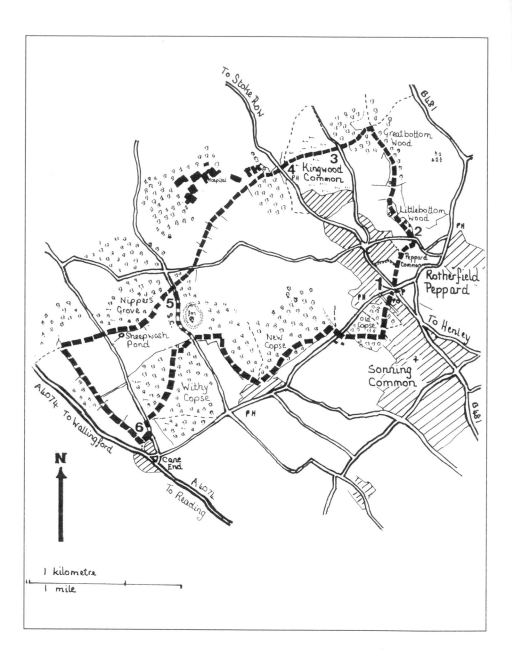

To Stoke Row

BL481

Great bottom Wood

Hospital

3

4 Kingwood Common
PH

Littlebottom Wood

2

PH

Peppard Common

1

Rotherfield Peppard

PH

Old Copse

To Henley

Nippers Grove

5

Sheepwash Pond

New Copse

Sonning Common

BL481

Withy Copse

PH

A4074 To Wallingford

6

Cane End

A 4074

To Reading

N

1 kilometre

1 mile

Peppard Common & Kingwood Common

7.5 miles   12 km

Short cut 5 miles   8 km

In the past, almost all this route would have been through commonland; today, unusually, much still remains along with old woodland and green lanes. It is fairly level apart from a short steep slope at the start and finish. Some bridleways may be very muddy after heavy rain.

Note. it is interesting to have the 1.25000 O.S. map on this walk as some features referred to in the text can be better seen on the map.

1. SU704813

Start from the car park opposite Peppard Common Post Office. Cross the Nettlebed/Henley road and take the path opposite, close to a Derestriction sign. Follow the path through trees to Peppard Common, bearing slightly left across the grass. After 100m at a crossing of paths, just before a gravel lane, go right downhill between trees and over grass, then left along the valley at the bottom until you reach a road.

Peppard Common is in the parish of Rotherfield Peppard; Anglo-Saxon "Rotherfield" meaning "open land where cattle graze". This open land here is probably

still similar in appearance to that of a thousand or
more years ago, the difference now being the
lack of grazing, which has led to the development
of thick growths of blackthorn and woodland.
In some places, this will be cleared by
conservationists to encourage growth of chalk loving
species.

The patches of heather and gorse at the top of the
slope are now rare examples in the Chilterns. However
this was typical vegetation on many commons here up
to about 150 years ago when the majority were enclosed
for agriculture (see Introduction). Both heather and gorse
were used by local people for fuel, with records of gorse
(furze) being planted for the purpose. Heather was also
used for thatching and bedding.

The varied geology of the common
is reflected in the different types of
vegetation to be found. The heather
and gorse grow in patches of sandy
acid soil, along with sheep's sorrel
and its taller relative common
sorrel. Both sorrels have
branched spikes of greenish
pink flowers and pear shaped
leaves. Their sharp tasting
leaves have long been used in
salads and sauces. In the
calcareous soil in the valley
bottom look for wild basil,
agrimony, burnet saxifrage and
lady's bedstraw. In early spring the
sloe or blackthorn bushes are covered
with white flowers, and in autumn are
purple with fruit.

The rich and varied flora provides
food plants for a large variety of
insects with many butterfly
species found here, including skippers, silver washed
fritillary, small copper, white
letter hairstreak and purple hairstreak.

Sheep's sorrel (left) and
common sorrel

Silver washed fritillary

2. SU706819

Cross the road and take the path opposite next to the field and gate. Walk through Littlebottom Wood, then between two fields, and straight on into Greatbottom Wood, following the white arrows. After 1km (0.6 miles), when you reach a junction of paths, turn left uphill with a field on the right, following the bridleway to a lane.

Both these woods are old; they look almost the same on Davis's map of 1797. Many plants to be seen along the bridleway reflect this long unbroken woodland history. Wood melick, a grass, has fresh green leaves with delicate reddish-brown sheathed single flowers. Several other plants here are named after their woodland origin - see how many you can spot, particularly in spring. In autumn, at the far edge of Littlebottom Wood, under the beech trees, you may find several types of toadstool fungi including the uncommon black and white caps of the aptly named magpie inkcap.

The hedge alongside the path linking the two woods

is substantial and so is a useful feature in the countryside. It enables small animals, birds, insects and even plants to move between the two wooded areas so increasing their populations of healthy wildlife.

Spindle is very obvious here in the autumn when its pink seed cases split to reveal bright orange seeds. Robins are among the birds that eat them.

In Greatbottom Wood notice the different types of ferns growing there. Bracken, probably the commonest fern in England, has fronds arising in a row from underground runners. Other ferns form clusters of fronds arising from a central base and can be distinguished by the shape of the individual segments of the lowest pair of leaflets (pinnae) as shown in the illustrations.

45 mins

3. SU698828

Fern pinnae: male (top), lady (centre) and buckler fern (bottom)

At the lane cross and follow the bridleway straight on through Kingwood Common to reach a small lane. Cross and continue in the same direction alongside a house to a road.

take right hand path

Kingwood Common is another with a long history. It was originally linked to Peppard Common before the intervening houses were built. It used to be called King

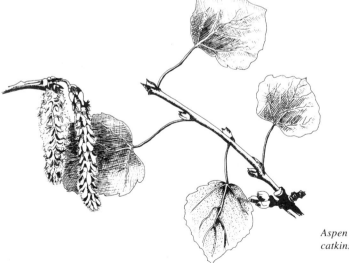

Aspen leaves and catkins

Wood Scrubbs, indicating the open scrubby heathland which existed up to the Second World War. Now the open nature has changed with colonisation by silver birch, aspen and oak, typical of recent woodland on poor soil. Aspen leaves on their long flattened stalks flutter in the slightest breeze, giving rise to the Latin name of *Populus tremula*, indicating this trembling motion. There are still a few small areas of heather remaining which are being encouraged by removal of bracken and silver birch to open the tree canopy and stimulate dormant heather seed to germinate (see Introduction).

The thick fallen leaves provide nutrients for fungi which can be seen in autumn. The familiar fly agaric has a bright red cap with white scales and spores are formed in the gills. It is poisonous, extracts were traditionally used as fly killer. The brownish caps of the boletus have spore lined pores and many types can be eaten, although some can lead to gastric upsets. Many of these attractive fungi are becoming rare due to over collecting, so it is best to leave them for others to enjoy as part of the autumn woodlands.

Fly agaric

During the 1939-45 war, huts were built on part of the common and used as a camp for the Royal Artillery, then later by the U.S. Army and eventually as a prisoner of war camp for German wounded. After the war it was home for Polish refugees and remains of concrete pathways and brick walls can still be seen.

4. SU692825

Cross the road and continue along the bridleway, initially lined with lamp posts and crossing another tarred road, for about 1km (0.75 miles). The buildings to your right were originally a hospital. When the bridleway reaches the road, turn right, then immediately left along the bridleway, taking the right branch.

Amongst the beech trees near the entrance to the former hospital, the descriptively named lawyer's wig fungus may be found in autumn. It is related to the magpie inkcap mentioned earlier; both fruiting bodies dissolve into an inky liquid to disperse their spores.

The bridleway, which you have followed for quite a distance from Kingwood Common, is one of the old routes over the Chilterns used formerly by drovers bringing their animals to High Wycombe or London

Lawyer's wig

from as far away as Wales. Kingwood Common was used as a resting place and a nearby pond opposite Nippers Grove is still called Sheepwash Pond.

Some of this track was part of the route between Henley and Goring used to speed the journey of goods by river. Boats were off loaded at Goring or Henley and goods taken by road between these towns to cut out a large loop of the Thames. Other sections of this route can be found in Walk 2.

5 SU682813

At another road cross and continue in the same direction along the woodland edge.

Old maps show that much of this landscape was open commonland in the past, the wooded areas remaining much the same. Indeed the trail continues through an area still called Whitewood Heath. Along the edge of Nippers Grove, plants can still be found which indicate acid soils and which are usually found on heathland. Heath speedwell has tiny lilac flowers and heart-shaped wrinkled leaves and wood sage has spikes of pale yellow flowers with leathery leaves similar to garden sage. Bracken and gorse are other such plants.

*(**Shorter route:** At the road, turn left and walk for about 500m until you reach a footpath to the left where you rejoin the main route in Point 6).*

Continue over the next road but at the end of the first field, turn left beside a cottage. Follow this path for about 1.5km or 1mile. At a stile close to a cottage, follow the path to another stile on to a lane.

As you walk along the path here, look out for another group of plants which indicate, not the type of soil, but its management. So-called weeds of cultivation grow, as their name suggests, where the ground is regularly

Wood sage

85

disturbed by agriculture. Nowadays most are eradicated by weedkiller but those on path or field edges escape. Mayweed, hedge mustard, fat hen and groundsel can all be seen here; their seeds are welcome food for small birds.

Past the plantation of Douglas firs, the fields on the left were woodland up until the late 19th century. Kempwood Cottage may indicate the lost name for this wood.

6. SU678799

At the lane turn left, then right after 150m beside a bungalow, May Lodge. Go through the gate and across the lawn to the wood where you turn left following the arrows on the trees. Follow the path through Withy Copse, crossing a large bank. At a staggered junction cross and go straight on. Take the right fork at the next junction, at the edge of the wood, again following arrows. At the road cross over.

(Short cut rejoins here)

Follow the path, parallel with the field edge, turning right at the arrow. Follow the path parallel with the field edge on your right, beside young trees, then through mature woodland. Close to the houses, take the right fork. Just before the road take the bridleway left parallel with the houses. Continue straight on, ignoring the lane beside the cottages. At the track at the end of the wood, turn right to the road.

The first wood here is Withy Copse and the two woods further on are also copses, New Copse and Old Copse. Originally this meant that the woods were managed as coppice, by cutting different parts of the wood on a rotation to "harvest" supplies of poles and other small sized wood. The banks which you see here and in other woods, often marked the boundaries between different areas of the copse and would be fenced when needed to prevent animals eating the new regrowth. This management gradually died out and now you see here even-aged beech trees, whose age can be estimated by measuring the girth at about chest height above the ground. (The span between your thumb and forefinger is about 6 inches or 15cm). Then every 1 inch or 2.5cm represents one year of growth, although trees crowded together on poor soils may grow more slowly.

On the edge of New Copse amongst the scrub you may smell bad drains, then find the fruiting bodies of the stinkhorn fungus with the highly descriptive Latin name of *Phallus impudicus*. It belongs to a group of fungi, which include the puffballs, whose spores are enclosed either within a thick skin or, as here, within a smelly greenish slimy tissue, which breaks down to free the tiny spores, eaten and dispersed by flies and slugs. The fruiting body first appears as a whitish ball, resembling an egg, before the spore-bearing stalk emerges. These "eggs" were considered to belong to alien demons and evil spirits, one of several legends associating stinkhorns with witchcraft. Further along this path some of the decaying conifer stumps are covered with the small golden antler-like fruiting bodies of the staghorn fungus.

7. SU698809

Cross over the road and enter the wood opposite, bearing left. Go over a stile and across the grass to a Woodland Trust sign. Go into the wood and follow the arrow to the right and further arrows through the wood. At a metal signpost turn left, eventually taking a gravel path leading downhill through a young conifer plantation to the road. Cross and take a path uphill between garden hedges to emerge opposite your starting point.

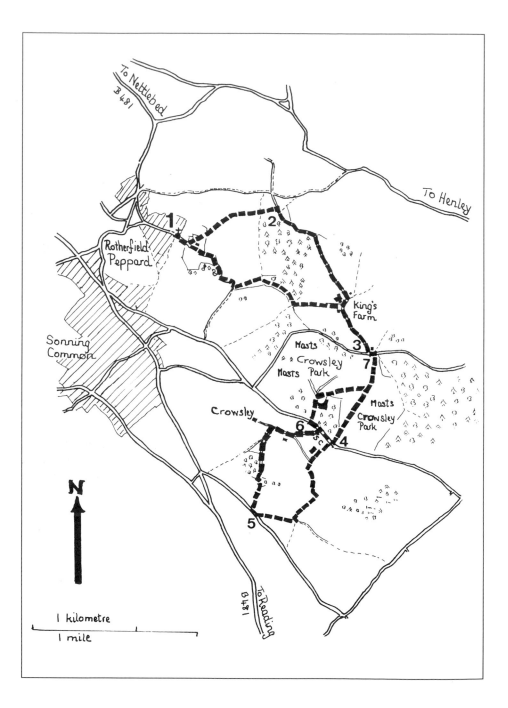

Rotherfield Peppard & Crowsley

7 miles   11 km

Short cuts 5 miles (8 km) and 3 miles (4.5 km)

This walk explores the countryside to the south-east of Rotherfield Peppard through an undulating landscape of lanes, woods and fields.

1. SU714815

Start at All Saints church and take the path leading alongside the churchyard. At the junction bear left over a stile, following a path between two fences. Over the next stile follow the path diagonally left across a large field. Over another stile go straight on through woodland to emerge onto a track.

This church, like most in England, has been extended and altered over the years. It originates from the Norman period with later additions, the last being the tower and vestry built in 1908. The churchyard contains old yew trees, a typical feature. There are many suppositions about why yew is associated with churchyards; yew is poisonous to animals so a churchyard was a safe place for this useful wood; some ancient specimens are thought to predate the Christian church in this country so may date back to a pagan use of the site. However,

Creeping buttercup (left)
and bulbous buttercup

the age of yews is often exaggerated so this latter
hypothesis may be untrue.

In spring the first field is bright with dandelions and
buttercups. Although dandelions attract insects, they are
actually self fertile. The pollen is not used for
fertilisation but to stimulate embryonic seed production,
a process called apomixis. Most of the buttercups here
are bulbous buttercups, identified by the sepals, which
protect the bud, bending back around the stalk
underneath the flower once it has opened. Creeping
buttercups look similar but the sepals are not folded
back.

As you cross the large field, the rolling landscape of
the Chiltern plateau is apparent, different to the steep
sided valleys to be seen further on (see Introduction).

This field may be long term set-aside, left with no
crops growing. At such times, many wild flowers grow
here, springing up from seeds lying dormant for several
years. Some species are now less common than they used
to be because of the use of selective herbicides which
kill them but not the cereal crops. Such wild plants which

Linnet

flower and seed at different times of the year, are vital food for numerous insects and birds. Apart from bees, butterflies, beetles and flies in spring and summer, look out for flocks of small finches in winter – goldfinch, linnets or chaffinches feeding on the seed heads.

Field pansy can be found here, a smaller version of the well known garden pansy. Its flowers are generally pale yellow but can be very variable to include blue or purple. You may also see masses of fumitory with small pink flowers and delicate greyish foliage which at a distance resembles smoke. If you pull up the plant it smells of smoke. Its medieval Latin name was *Fumus terrae* meaning smoke of the earth.

Notice the ghost hedge across the field marked by a line of isolated trees to the right. Removal of hedges has been common since the advent of large agricultural machinery which is more efficient to use in large fields. This has been a loss, not only to wildlife for food and security, but also to the local landscape which has changed in many places in the Chilterns from being small scale and almost secret to rather open and featureless. The recent increase in numbers of trees planted along field edges or in corners has been encouraged by wildlife conservationists.

Common fumitory

The sandy soil of the path is used by solitary bees for

their nesting sites. In early spring you may notice numerous small holes surrounded by small mounds of soil. The bees will close the hole once it has been stocked with sufficient food and the eggs have been laid. The larvae develop underground and then emerge as adults the following year to start a new colony (see Harpsden Walk 7).

This woodland is not old; that on the left is less than 30 years old as the 1973 Ordnance Survey map shows it as open ground then. The area to the right was open ground when the 1st edition Ordnance Survey map was surveyed in 1830. It is likely that these trees were planted at the end of the 19th century at a time of agricultural depression when crops were not profitable. Notice the large oak trees to the right, but few large trees on the left in the younger woodland. The path is lined with Scots pines; notice the characteristic orange bark at the top of the trunks. To the right, numerous sycamore saplings may in time replace many of the oaks in the wood because of their vigourous growth.

On the path look out for hazelnut shells. Those with irregular holes have been eaten by voles, those broken in half have been eaten by grey squirrels, whose nests or drays can be seen at the top of the pine trees.

2. SU724818

At the track turn right and continue for almost 1km (0.7 mile). At a junction turn right and carry on along Kings Farm Lane to the road.

Human influence on woodland and hedges are very clear to see. Laurel has been planted, probably for cover for game birds, while non-native conifers are present in the woodland. The oak woodland changes abruptly to beech, showing a change in management regimes or ownership. Where the trees have been cleared, there are large patches of purple foxgloves, bluebells and yellow St John's wort, which like cooler moister conditions than the fields crossed earlier. The hedges bordering the track contain hazel growing from several stems. This shows that it has been repeatedly cut in the past for a supply of

Kings Farm Lane

long slender wood used for woven fencing, bean poles and other uses around the farm and garden. The oldest feature can be seen on the left. Look for a marked bank which veers off to the left as the path curves to the right. This marks the parish boundary between Rotherfield Peppard and Rotherfield Greys and marks an ancient system of administration predating the Norman invasion in 1066 but which is still relevant today.

At Kings Farm, notice the barn on the right which has been converted into a house. This use, while reflecting the changes in farming practice and needs, preserves vernacular buildings which otherwise would fall into decay.

(**SHORT CUT 1**: *For a shorter walk, turn right along the footpath beside Kingsfield House and follow the directions from Point 7 back to the start*).

The verges of the lane here are full of flowers in early summer with white cow parsley, tall spikes of great mullein and pink flowered storksbill. Occasionally you may hear the high pitched squealing of shrews from the undergrowth. These tiny mouse-like animals can be recognised by their long noses. The small size means that they lose body heat rapidly so have to eat almost continuously when awake. In cool conditions they die in a few hours if they have insufficient food.

As the lane starts to descend, notice the hedges on each side which were laid in 1996. A thick barrier is formed by cutting the tree trunks almost through, then laying them sideways at an angle. New shoots spring up from the cut bases so that there are no gaps in the hedge. This is a skilled craft not often seen today, as it is easier to fill a gap with a few strands of wire. In many old hedges you can see old slanting stems, although if not laid on a regular basis the hedge will become thin and gappy.

At the end of the lane notice another fine old barn at Old Place, an old building dating in parts from the 16th century. The barn however has been brought here and reconstructed.

The Old Place

3. SU732804

At the road turn left then take the footpath to the right up wooden steps. The path leads uphill over grassland and continues over level ground between the clumps of trees. Eventually you will reach a stile leading onto a road at the far right-hand corner of the park alongside a wood.

This area is Crowsley Park, enclosed in the time of James II when 250 acres (110ha) were surrounded by a fence of split oak.

The grassland is interesting as the soil conditions change as you walk uphill. At the bottom plants which like chalky (calcareous) soil can be found such as salad burnet, stemless thistle and cowslips. At the top of the slope chalk intolerant (calcifuge) plants grow like gorse, tormentil and sheep's sorrel, indicating that the chalk is covered by a layer of sandy acid soil. Heather may have grown here in the past as it does in similar circumstances not far from here (see Walk 5 Peppard Common and Kingwood Common).

95

The short turf favours the development of anthills which are scattered across the slope. Ants bring soil to the surface as they tunnel so producing mounds, which increase in size over the years if undisturbed by farming activity. The fine soil acts as an excellent seed bed and suits plants which prefer open ground free from vigourous competing vegetation. One such plant found here is the changing forget-me-not, a small flowered species whose pale yellow flowers gradually turn blue. Buck rabbits use anthills as vantage points; their droppings contain seeds which quickly germinate in the fine soil.

Notice the BBC radio masts and dishes to your right, well hidden from the surrounding area by the landform and trees.

This parkland is very different from the agricultural landscape surrounding it. There are no hedges or fields; the ornamental trees were planted to enhance the view and to reflect the wealth and status of the owner. Originally Crowsley Park was noted for its seven avenues of trees, parts of which still remain as substantial oaks. To the left of the route is a clump of sweet chestnut trees, which can be easily identified even in winter by the spiral pattern of the bark on the trunk. Despite the size of these trees, the wood is not good for planks as it has natural cracks or "shakes". When used for making paling for fences the trees are coppiced and the growth cut after about 12 years. In England the nuts only ripen in the south after a good summer. On the right is a group of lime trees which have obvious dark clusters on the branches. This is mistletoe, which is partly parasitic on the trees. Mistletoe is becoming rare because of the demand for it at Christmas. It used to grow in old orchards but a decline in fruit growing and modern cultivation methods means that it is now an infrequent partner.

Changing forget-me-not

4. SU729795

(**SHORT CUT 2**: *Turn right along the road for about 400m to rejoin the main walk at Point 6*).

At the road cross over and take the path opposite across the corner of the field. Over another stile turn right along the track, following the path around the left edge of the buildings and continuing along the field edge down and uphill. Bear left keeping the hedgebank to the right, then at a stile turn right. Follow the path with the hedge on the left. At a Junction, take the path to the far right along the hedge line to emerge beside brick cottages.

Notice the hedge along the track before the farm buildings. It is trimmed to an A-shape, which encourages growth at the base of the hedge. Its shape ensures that it is strong and can withstand heavy snowfall.

The cultivated fields are a contrast to the open parkland just walked through. The regular cycle of ploughing, sowing and harvesting means that the wild flowers do not have the permanence of those in the park grassland. The hedgeline facing you as you walk downhill marks the boundary between Shiplake and Eye and Dunsden parishes. Notice how this hedge is growing on a pronounced bank, more visible in winter, which emphasises its importance.

The thatched half timbered cottage to the left on the road is an older building than the brick cottages closer to the path. Thatch for roofing was later superseded by

Cottage, Crowsley Park House

tiles or slates while the coloured brick patterns show that these cottages are probably Victorian.

5. SU721788

Turn right along the road for about 100m, then right again over the stile. Cross the field to another stile and into the wood. Follow the white arrows through the wood, then follow the path uphill along the wood edge and then along a field boundary. Continue straight on until you reach the lane. Here turn right beside a black and white cottage and walk along the lane, bearing left at a junction. At the road turn left and walk 100m to the entrance of Crowsley Park where you turn right.

As you cross the field to the wood, notice the variety of colours in the landscape which reflect the diverse crops and land usage. The yellow of oil seed rape is now a familiar sight but the pale blue of linseed is not so frequent. Silage, hay and cereal crops all have different colours and all vary with the seasons. In winter many of these fields are likely to be green, rather than the bare earth of ploughed land as, nowadays, crops tend to be sown in autumn instead of spring.

Both the thatched Frieze Cottage here and the one seen earlier appear on a map made by Richard Davis in 1797, as do the woods just walked through. The path leading to the brick cottages was shown as a track, but by the 1830's it was shown as a dead end, and did not extend as far as the present day path.

6. SU727796

(Short cut 2 rejoins here). **At Crowsley Park, turn right into the park through the gates beside the lodge and walk up the drive. Just past the house, turn right through a gate, follow the signs which lead you eventually to the parkland beside the mistletoe bearing trees seen earlier. Retrace your steps through the park and downhill to emerge close to Old Place again.**

Crowsley Park House

The present Crowsley Mansion has gothic battlements and turrets which were added to the 18th century building in 1800. This building replaced an earlier mansion built between 1685-8 at the same time as the park was created. The house is flanked by two large conifers, both magnificent specimens of 19th century introductions to Britain. On the right the giant redwood, with reddish fibrous bark, originates from the Sierra Nevada mountains in California where they can grow to over 300 feet (100m). In Britain the tallest is only about 135 feet. Obviously these trees are too large to grow anywhere other than landscaped grounds and

99

parks. The spreading cedar tree can also grow to a large size but with massive trunks, the largest of which can be 40 feet in circumference in their natural surroundings. Lebanon cedar comes from mountainous regions of Syria and Lebanon where the largest are thought to be about 2000 years old.

As you walk back across the park, notice the typical shape of the parkland trees. These trees have their lower branches grazed by animals producing a straight edge or browse line at grazing height. Most trees growing in the "wild" have a more natural irregular appearance.

7. SU733804

At the road, turn left then right up Kings Farm Lane until you reach a path beside Kingsfield House on the left. *(Short Cut 1 rejoins here).* **Take this path and after about 100m cross a stile and turn right into another field before reaching a woodland edge. Continue downhill, turning right at the bottom taking a path through the woodland. Over two stiles, turn left along a bridleway marked with a blue arrow and with a fence on the left. At a junction continue straight on along a path following the field edge. At the top of the hill the path crosses a woodland strip and turns right along a field edge. Over the next stile turn left to return to the church.**

The field edges at the beginning of this section contain many flowering plants including greater knapweed and hardheads (which look similar but the latter has smaller flower heads), St John's wort, weld, wild basil, agrimony and hedge bedstraw. Many plants have long been used in folk medicine, but modern research is now showing that these remedies are as effective as modern drugs. St John's wort preparations have been used as anti-depressants in German-speaking countries for many years but only recently has it had clinical trials in Britain. It is likely to be developed as a low cost treatment with few side effects for this condition. The woodland edge also contains many plants, including sanicle and wood spurge indicating that it is an old wood. Unlike the woods at the start of the walk (Point 1) woodland is shown here on the map of Oxfordshire made in 1797. This does not mean that the present trees date from that period or earlier but it is likely there has been constant woodland cover for several centuries and the land has not been used for cultivation. As the path leads into the wood there are planted Scots pines and other conifers, but the conditions are open enough to allow foxgloves, honeysuckle and ferns to grow along the path.

Out of the wood, the path leads along the edge of a small valley. The bank to the left across the valley is another parish boundary this time between Rotherfield Peppard and Harpsden parishes.

Notice how chalky the soil is along this part of the walk, so much so that, not far away, the continuation of this valley is called Stony Bottom.

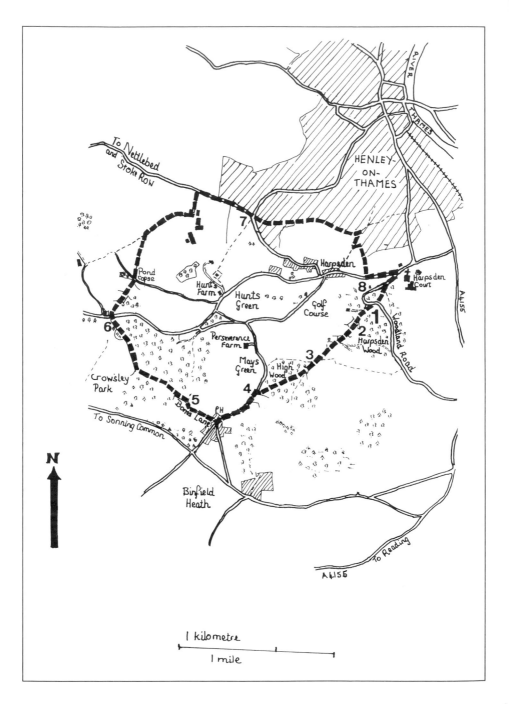

N

To Nettlebed
and Stoke Row

HENLEY-
ON-
THAMES

RIVER THAMES

Harpsden

7

Pond
Copse

Hunt's
Farm

Hunts
Green

Golf
Course

Harpsden
Court

8

1

2

Harpsden
Wood

Woodland Road

A4155

6

Perseverance
Farm

Mays
Green

High
Wood

3

Crowsley
Park

5

Bones Lane

4

P.H.

To Sonning Common

Binfield
Heath

To Reading

A4155

1 kilometre

1 mile

Harpsden

5.5 miles   9 km

This walk encircles the parish of Harpsden and is a fairly level walk except for two short climbs.

1. SU760806

Start at the top of Woodland Road, just past the steepest climb, from lay-byes next to Woodland Trust signs. Facing away from Harpsden church, take the path on the right which very soon joins a stony track along the edge of Harpsden Wood. (Take care here as there are several paths leading into the woodland – if in doubt, go back along the road for 100m and take the track directly). Along the track, bear right at a junction, past a house called Pen-y-Bryn, then over a stile close to Harpsden Wood Grange.

Harpsden Wood is managed by the Woodland Trust, an organisation which seeks to safeguard woods in the landscape, protect them as habitats for wildlife and allow free access for quiet recreation. This typical beechwood has very little ground cover except for brambles which spread vigorously as the stems take root wherever they touch the ground. Unlike brambles in sunny hedgerows, these have few flowers or fruit. Bluebells may be seen in spring, growing and flowering before the beech leaves cast a deep shade.

Plants grown in gardens alongside the track have often escaped into the nearby woodland. Portuguese laurel is a favourite hedging plant as it tolerates shade and forms a thick barrier. Its crushed leaves produce poisonous fumes and were used in sealed jars by insect collectors and entomologists to kill their specimens.

Alongside Harpsden Wood Grange look on the right for a line of hornbeam trees. The leaves are similar to beech but have more pronounced veins; the tree is in fact related to hazel. The wood is very hard and resistant to mechanical wear. It was used for cogs, screws, rollers and pulley blocks and was also coppiced for firewood.

2. SU758804

The path goes over the next stile, under low branches of hornbeam. Go straight on along the field edge then left at the fence to a third stile beside an oak tree. Walk diagonally right across the next field to another stile beside the corner of a garden. Follow the path, with the garden hedge on your left, to a final stile on to a rough lane where you turn right.

Hornbeam leaf

Leaving the woodland, the landscape becomes open and quite flat, part of the plateau which forms the typical Chiltern landscape.

Some hedges have been removed, leaving only a thin line of trees. Riding is a popular pastime in this area and fields here and elsewhere have been subdivided with wooden post and rail fences for horse paddocks. Cattle or sheep need thicker barriers like hedges or walls. When hedges cease to be managed they grow tall and straggly with gaps at the base – notice the hedgeline across the centre of the field to your right. The mixed species produce a swathe of colour as different species come into leaf and flower in the spring and then change again in autumn. Such hedges act as a link between areas of woodland, providing important shelter and perches for birds, many of which do not like to fly across expanses of open fields.

Beech leaf

As you cross the fields, notice the rich grass growing here. These improved grasslands produce hay and silage crops and the lush growth tends to eliminate many smaller flowering plants. This contrasts with less improved grazing land to be seen later in the walk and which contains colourful mixtures of flowers.

As you walk alongside the garden on your left, notice the three colours of the bluebells in spring. The pink and white colours are inherited colours of the usual blue form and are less attractive to insects, so reducing the chances of successful pollination and seed production. These varieties are therefore much less common where they occur.

As you climb the final stile, look at the left end of the large field behind you. Notice the slight regular undulations of old ridge-and-furrow ploughing. This is not common in the Chilterns and probably means that this immediate area was farmed as large open fields, rather than more usual smaller enclosed fields. Ridge and furrow aided drainage, and although this land is on a high plateau, the mixed soil conditions here, often with thick clay, may have benefited from such management. You will soon see ground conditions which indicate that this was quite possible.

3. SU754799

Turn right along the lane and beside Highwood House take the path straight on, following the bridleway into High Wood. 10m into the wood take the right fork, following the arrow on the tree. Continue along this path through the wood, passing newly planted areas and beside water filled hollows along the track to the far side of the wood. At the road turn left.

The often wet nature of the ground on the plateau is shown here by the presence of soft rush. The spiky "leaves" of this plant are really stems and bear tufts of brownish flowers which would never grow on a leaf.

Soft rush Further along the path are large puddles which rarely dry out completely. Look out for the two-toed footprints of deer and the three spreading toeprints of pheasant.

The woodland here is different to the beechwood seen earlier. Here sycamore, ash and oak are common as well as areas of conifer planting. New planting contains beech, oak and cherry, although silver birch has invaded the open ground. This tree, named after its attractive bark, produces light, wind-blown seeds and hence is a natural early coloniser of open ground and serves to nurse other species such as oak. Its twigs were used for making besom brooms, used in the garden and in folklore by witches!

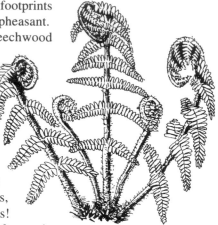

Male fern

The mixture of trees produce different leaf canopies and shapes, allowing some light to reach the woodland floor, so there is a good mix of plants growing at ground level. Several species of ferns can be seen, their fronds uncurling to form the characteristic crosier shape as they grow in spring.

Each season has obvious variations in colour and temperature but pause to notice the smell as well. In spring the air is sweet with bluebells, in summer resin from conifers is aromatic and in autumn the fallen leaves produce the characteristic "wood" smell.

As you approach the end of the wood close to the road, look to the wood edge on the left and notice the large bank which marks the parish boundary between Harpsden and Shiplake.

Look at the exposed soil here as well. It is full of rounded pebbles, different to the sharp edged flints more usually found in the Chilterns. Their shape indicates that they have been worn away by water; an ancient route of the Thames is thought to have flowed in this vicinity between present day Caversham and Henley.

4. SU748796

Turn left along the road until you reach a track, Bones Lane, to the right in front of the Bottle and Glass pub. Follow the track to reach woodland.

The road is bordered to the left by a very mixed hedge – see how many species you can find – but a little further on, the remaining section of hedge to the right is almost entirely elm. This may suggest that the two hedges have different origins, the elm being more recent than the mixed hedge which could date from the distant past when the woodland was cleared for fields. However the elm hedge could have developed as suckers from old elm trees in a previously mixed hedge, so long ago that the original elm stumps have gone.

The houses mark the edge of Binfield Heath (see Walk 8)which is noted in the name of the road opposite – Common Road. The pub, the Bottle and Glass was originally the farmhouse of Bournes Farm dating from the late medieval period. It was first recorded in 1678 and became a public house in 1764. Family names of some previous occupants can be seen scratched on the old glass in some of the windows.

Along the track the large dead stumps are elm. They indicate how the landscape altered during the 1970's with the loss of so many substantial hedgerow trees. Yellow lesser celandine flowers can be seen in early spring. The flowers and leaves die back quickly so that

*The Bottle and Glass
public house*

Lesser celandines

by May there is no sign of them; the plants survive as fleshy roots underground during the summer and autumn.

5. SU741795

Bear left into the wood and continue on the bridle-way, following arrows, then uphill to reach an iron fence along the edge of parkland. The bridleway continues along this and eventually meets the road.

As you walk through the woods look for several examples of old saw pits. These were dug in many places in the Chiltern woods so that timber could be cut on site rather than transported as logs (see Introduction). A much larger hollow to the left of the bridleway is a swallow hole, formed when a undergound hole in the underlying chalk collapsed, leaving a hollow on the surface. It could be confused with a quarry for extracting chalk or flint but all the sides are steep with no obvious means of exit for materials.

Different groups of trees grow here, each with a distinctive effect on the landscape. Beech has the typical bare ground as seen earlier whereas the more open oak, ash and sycamore have more undergrowth. The small areas of broad leaved woodland are old and were marked with banks, some of which are still visible, particularly to the left of the track. The broadleaved trees contrast with the coniferous spruce, larch and Douglas fir which are planted as a quick growing timber crop. Conifers are cone-bearing trees and different species have

European larch

Douglas fir

Norway spruce

characteristic cones. Douglas fir has large cones with obvious three-toothed scales forming a pattern on them, but larch cones are smaller. Larch is deciduous, losing its leaves in winter; it also drops many branches and twigs which can be seen on the ground beneath the trees. The name spruce is derived from the German *sprossen* – a sprout which refers to its numerous short branches.

The iron railings follow the boundary of Crowsley Park which you can cross in Walk 6; originally the boundary was marked by a fence of split oak. The park can be seen well from here, the groups of large trees scattered across the grass, different to the landscape of fields and woods seen elsewhere. Some of the trees are the remnants of the seven avenues which radiated from the house to meet the alternate elms and oaks planted around the edge of the park. At North Lodge two more large conifers, cedars with spreading horizontal branches, grow at each side of the gate.

6. SU733804

When you reach the road, turn right for 10m and take the path to the left uphill. Follow it to a stile, then continue as before, diagonally right on the grassy path to another stile, onto a lane.

As you cross the first field, note the line of lime trees in the garden to the left. Lime is a native British tree but in most places has disappeared from woodlands. It has a soft white wood used for fine carving while the fibrous inner bark was often used in the making of birch besoms, to tie the twigs together. Lime can tolerate regular trimming and is often seen as a roadside tree in suburban areas.

The lane leading downhill is almost unchanged from that shown on an estate map made in 1586, now held in the Oxfordshire Archives; its age is shown by the steep banks on each side. The lane leads to Hunt's Farm, the last survivor of a small settlement shown here on the same map. The outlying farms and fields here are still essentially little changed from the landscape of enclosed fields and woods shown then, although some hedges have been removed and some new houses built. Harpsden is an old scattered settlement mentioned in the Domesday Book of 1086. Its name means harp-shaped valley and is a good description of the curving shape of the valley eastwards from here.

Cross the lane and take the footpath opposite to a junction with another footpath. Bear right for about 400m and at a hedgeline turn right towards some houses. At the houses turn left along the road. Turn right at the main road, Greys Road, and continue to the junction.

Where the path levels out across the last two fields, the land to the left beyond the large buildings, has an ancient history as the site of a palaeolithic flint "factory". The earliest human inhabitants of the Upper Thames valley between 125,000 and 70,000 years ago left their mark here in a loop of the ancient Thames before the last Ice Age. The river was an easy route for people to follow and many archaeological sites are found along river routes.

7. SU747814

At the junction with Gillot's Road continue ahead along a bridleway. When you reach a junction of paths take the middle one with a wooden fence on your left. Continue along the edge of the houses until you reach a footpath on the right signed to Harpsden. Follow this, after a short distance turning left along a residential road. After 25m turn right to follow a lane down hill. At the road turn left and walk with care.

Although quite urban in nature, this type of area still provides habitats for wildlife. Some wild plants still survive here like cow parsley and nettles, while others have escaped from nearby gardens such as cultivated yellow archangel with silvery patches on the leaves or purple flowered honesty which later has circular seed heads. When these are ripe, the outer cover peels off to reveal a shiny white membrane which gives rise to its other name of moonwort. Some plants here are shade tolerant like ivy which trails over the ground and up tree trunks, others flower early in the season before the trees cast too much shade. Cow parsley is taller here than in full sun, as are nettles which also produce larger, more delicate leaves.

The fields to the right are yellow in spring with dandelion flowers, a contrast to the improved grassland passed earlier.

Down the lane, past the last houses, the hedges are thick and overgrown with hawthorn, cherry, dog rose and bramble. These are a rich source of flowers, fruit and berries at different times of the year, providing food and shelter for nesting birds, mammals and insects.

8. SU759808

Turn left at the road, passing a golf course to the right, followed by a cemetery. At the junction turn right into Woodland Road and take the path to the left uphill amongst the trees, parallel to the road. At a junction of paths, take the right fork to return to the start.

The landscape of the golf course contrasts with both the flowery grassland and the improved fields. The scattered trees are reminiscent of the parkland seen earlier but the smooth greens and sand bunkers bring an urban feel to the landscape. The flower rich margins are good for wildlife but the heavy use of pesticides on the greens and tees counteracts this benefit.

As you walk uphill notice the exposed soil at the base of several trees blown over by the wind. The chalk and flint are close to the surface here, different to the clay at the top of the plateau. Look on the soil around the exposed roots for numerous small holes where solitary bees tunnel to make their individual nests. Although solitary in that they do not live in communal hives, these insects are often found living in close proximity when conditions, such as suitable soil, are right. On sunny spring days, many of these small fly-like bees can be seen around these nesting sites (see Walk 6).

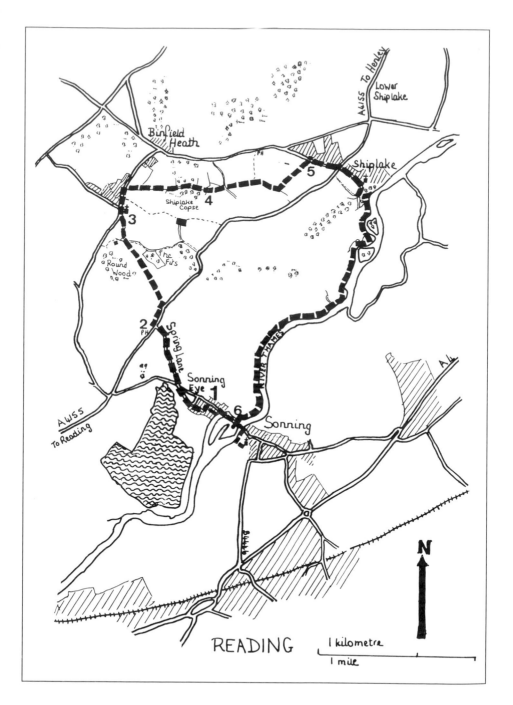

Binfield
Heath

A4155 To Henley

Lower
Shiplake

5

Shiplake

4

Shiplake
Copse

3

The
Firs

Round
Wood

2
PH

Spring Lane

Sonning
Eye

1

RIVER THAMES

A4155
To Reading

6

Sonning

A4

N

READING

1 kilometre

1 mile

Sonning Eye & Shiplake

6 miles   10 km

Initially walking on roads, some busy, the route soon climbs gently away from the Thames, following green lanes and footpaths. The river is reached at Shiplake and followed back to the start. The going is easy throughout this walk.

1. SU750760

Start from Sonning Eye, close to the entrance to Reading Sailing Club, reached from the side turning off the roundabout on the main road. Walk away from the village to reach a gate at the end of the disused through-road. Cross the main road into Spring Lane opposite, marked "No Entry". After about 100m cross a stile on the right and walk along the left edge of the field parallel to the road.

Sonning Eye is named from the Old English word for island or dry land surrounded by marsh. A little further on, it is obvious, even now, that the latter was the case in the past. There are several small streams and damp areas, which then would have been less controlled so that all the low lying land here would have been waterlogged for at least part of the year. Such factors would have influenced land use as wet meadows would only be useful for summer grazing, the animals being moved to higher ground in the wetter winter months.

Spring Lane has a mass of interesting hedgerow plants. Snowberry has tiny pink flowers which are highly sought after by bees for nectar. Introduced from America, the plant gets its name from the white waxy berries produced in autumn. Hops trail over the hawthorn branches and guelder rose with flat heads of white flowers occurs occasionally. Along the fieldpath you will find the tall slender stems of wall lettuce with yellow flowers. This is a member of the daisy (Compositae) family – look for other members along the route such as hawkbit, sow thistle, chicory with blue flowers and dandelion. The ground dried roots of the latter two are still used as coffee substitutes.

Where the path rejoins the road, there is an area of recent tree planting opposite. Many of the species chosen here reflect the damp nature of the ground; alder, willow and aspen all prefer moist conditions.

2. SU747768

At the main road, cross with care and go up the wooden steps opposite. Turn right and follow the permissive path to the top of the rise. Here go left and take the bridleway. Follow this track, going straight on at the junction, for about 1km (0.5 miles), until it reaches a road and houses.

The busy road is soon left behind as the track gradually climbs uphill. The verges are full of wild flowers in summer and are good examples of unimproved calcareous grassland. The poor soil discourages growth of lush grasses so that flowers can thrive without much competition for light or nutrients. Plants like marjoram, greater knapweed, wild basil and rest harrow all have pink or purple flowers while meadow cranesbill, field scabious and self heal are blue or mauve.

Chicory

The path passes between Round Wood and The Firs; notice that as the track becomes more shady, the flowering plants disappear. Pause here to look back at the view over the Thames valley with the A4 visible in the distance and the buildings of Reading to the right.

Notice that in this area there is a wet flush in the field to the right and a tiny stream in the woodland on the left. The grass may be greener and taller and there are clumps of rushes. These are localised springs, occurring where ground water meets an impervious layer such as clay. Local geology can be very mixed so that even though you have just climbed a chalky slope where you would expect springs to flow at the base, here water emerges above the chalk. Remember the name of the pub at the main road – The Flowing Spring!

3. SU743779

At the road turn right past houses then, after about 300m, take the path to the right signed Shiplake. Follow this path along a field edge then through woodland.

This village is Binfield Heath, a collection of houses scattered round the remains of the common land. The name Binfield indicates that this area, like Rotherfield, was so named in Anglo-Saxon times because of its open landscape on well-drained poor sandy or pebbly soil, contrasting with the wooded nature of the surrounding area on wetter clay-with-flints. Looking at the Ordnance Survey map, Gravel Road and Sandpit Lane can be seen, giving an indication of the soil here.

Many houses here are Victorian, some built of red brick without the familiar flints. The Congregational Chapel was built in 1835, probably around the time that houses were built here. However, if you go on about 150m beyond the footpath sign you will find Hollow Tree Cottage, a half-timbered and thatched cottage, a rare survivor of one of several labourer's dwellings built on the edge of the Heath.

As the path approaches the woodland, it is overhung

by cherry trees which provide a tasty snack during late July. In spring, the trees are covered in white blossom, a typical sight in the Chilterns. In the woods you may also find wild raspberries and redcurrants, the latter possibly being a garden escape.

In the woodland, Shiplake Copse, notice the very obvious bank alongside the track. This bank marks the boundary between the parishes of Shiplake on the left and Eye and Dunsden to the right. Like the parishes along the Chiltern escarpment, those here tend to be quite long and narrow so that they encompass both low lying fertile riverside land and wooded hilly ground. This variation in soil and conditions were very important in the past when villages tended to be mostly self sufficient. Hereabouts there are three areas of woodland with "Shiplake" in their names. This is the only copse, meaning that it was managed as coppice, and even now evidence of this can be seen. Hazel was cut to nearly ground level every 15 to 20 years, which stimulated regrowth of many stems. Oaks were left to grow into large trees, standards, the timber eventually being used for building or ship construction. Here, on the right, many standard oaks can be seen, while on the left a different management regime has planted rhododendrons, probably as cover for game birds. The more open nature of the coppiced areas would have allowed woodland plants to flower. Bluebells can be seen here in the spring, but it is likely that the cover is now too dense for many others to grow.

4. SU752781

Out of the wood, the path bears left uphill passing an overgrown pit on the left, then across a field towards a large silver birch tree. Continue straight on over an old track and another field towards a telegraph pole. At the post follow the path left then at the next pole, continue for another 100m to another signpost. Here turn right with a wire fence on your left. Go left over a stile and then straight on to a kissing gate then left to the road.

5. SU762784

At the road, turn right and continue to the main road. Cross this with care and take Church Lane opposite. Follow this past the church, then at a junction of tracks, bear right downhill, then left at the next junction of paths. When you reach the river, turn right to cross a footbridge beside a boat house, then follow the riverbank path to Sonning.

Shiplake Church dates from the 12th century but was heavily restored in 1869 by G.E. Street for the Phillimore family, important landowners in the area still. Many of the headstones in the churchyard are memorials to family members who were prominent in the Royal Navy, the judiciary and the church.

The church yard contains many fine specimens of evergreen trees, including yew, cedar of Lebanon with branches forming horizontal layers of foliage, and the deodar cedar whose branches tend to turn slightly downwards.

Church of St. Peter and St. Paul, Shiplake

When you reach the river pause to look over the bridge beside the boathouse. This slow moving stream entering the Thames is home to yellow water lilies. The bright yellow flowers emerge above the water surface in order to be pollinated by small flies. They are not true lilies, which are all land plants, but belong to the buttercup

family. The lily family include native plants like lily-
of-the-valley, fritillary, ramsons and bluebell. They all
have only three sepals and three petals, which are of
similar shape, colour and size, so giving the appearance
of a six-petalled flower.

The river bank path is part of the newly designated
Thames Long Distance Path which leads from the
source of the river at Thames Head near Cirencester
through London to the Thames Barrier. The river bank
is rich in plants which are adapted to damp or
waterlogged soil. In summer you will find flowers
of valerian, meadow rue, water dropwort, comfrey
and marsh woundwort. Meadow rue has incon-
spicuous flowers whose stamens are long and
yellow, giving the flowers their colour. It is
typically found in damp hay meadows, but is
uncommon now as most riverside meadows have
been drained and improved in recent decades. Valerian
is a tallish plant with clusters of small pale pink flowers
and is related to the brighter red valerian seen on cliffs
and walls. It is used in herbal medicine to relieve nervous
tension and insomnia. Its name reflects its medicinal
properties, being derived from the latin "valere"
meaning to be healthy.

Meadow rue

During midsummer you are likely to glimpse
both swallows and sand martins swooping low
over the water and grass to catch flying insects.
Although swallows nest in many different places
such as house eaves, barns or under bridges, sand
martins live in tunnels bored in sand or gravel pits or
in eroded river banks. They are likely to be
nesting in the nearby gravel pits
between Sonning and Reading. The
light brown martins with blunt
forked tails are easily
distinguished from the larger dark
blue swallows with deeply forked tails.

There are also numerous plants of the white flowered
horseradish with large dock-like leaves. Introduced to
Britain from southern Europe about 400 years ago, it
has escaped from gardens and very successfully estab-

Water dropwort

River Thames near Shiplake

lished itself by roadsides and in uncultivated areas. Horseradish sauce made from the root of the plant is the tasty traditional accompaniment to roast beef, but peeling and grating the roots causes copious eye-watering due to the acrid mustard oil released!

Great crested grebes are frequently seen on the river now, even though they were virtually exterminated in the 19th century when their bright feathers were much used to decorate hats. Their reversal in fortune occurred due to the formation of flooded gravel pits in the Thames valley and elsewhere, which provided breeding sites, in conjunction with their conservation by the bird protection movement promoted by the Royal Society for the Protection of Birds (RSPB) founded in 1889.

6. SU755758

Cross a wooden footbridge to emerge on the main
road. *(See below for detour into Sonning.)*

Turn right along the road, passing Sonning Mill,
and cross the river to reach the French Horn Hotel.
Here turn left and follow the marked footpath along
a tarmac path, bearing right at Furleigh Cottages.
At the junction turn left back to the start.

Sonning Mill would have been a valuable asset to the
area as a corn mill; it is now used as a theatre, and instead
is a valuable cultural resource.

The path through Sonning Eye passes a variety of
buildings of different ages and styles, the changes in
building materials reflecting the gradual change from
the use of local materials such as timber and clay, brick-
and-flint to mass-produced modern materials. Notice

Sonning Bridge

St. Andrew's Church, Sonning

also how some dwellings have been converted from redundant farm buildings, so that the character of the village is retained, although the use of the buildings has changed.

TO VISIT SONNING: Turn left along the road and over the bridge. Here you can walk up the road past houses and hotels, or continue for a short distance right, along the Thames Path, then left to St Andrew's church. To return to the start retrace your steps to the end of the wooden footbridge and continue as above.

Sonning is an attractive village with many half timbered or brick and flint houses. The present brick bridge dates from the late 18th century but the earlier one is thought to have been here during the reign of Henry VIII. Look for the plaque on the bridge marking the ancient boundary between Oxfordshire and Berkshire which follows the line of the River Thames. St Andrew's church was restored during the 19th century but there are remnants of earlier periods dating back to Anglo-

Saxon times. Sonning used to be part of the diocese of
Ramsbury in Wiltshire and the Bishop's Palace stood
close to the church until the 16th century. The wall and
arch close to the main entrance of the church bear a
plaque explaining that the bricks came from London
houses bombed during the Second World War.

Acknowledgements

This book was written and researched by Mary Webb,
Alan Spicer and Allister Smith, all of Oxford Brookes
University, and was illustrated by Louise Spicer.

The authors are grateful for help from the staff of the
Countryside Service of the Oxfordshire County Council
and the Centre for Oxfordshire Studies and to Dr. Alan
Childs of Oxford Brookes University for advice on the
geology of the area.

The project was sponsored by the Council for the
Protection of Rural England, Oxfordshire County
Council, South Oxfordshire District Council, The Rover
Group and Oxford Brookes University.

South Oxfordshire
District Council

OXFORD
BROOKES
UNIVERSITY

CPRE

Your countryside
Your voice

CPRE *Membership*

Return completed forms to
**CPRE, FREEPOST,
GOLDTHORPE,
ROTHERHAM S63 9BR**

Name

Address

Postcode

☐ Yes, I want to help CPRE's work for our countryside. Please enrol me as a member as indicated below *(tick as appropriate)*

SUBSCRIPTIONS

☐ Individual	£17.50	☐ Affiliated organisation	£17.50
☐ Joint	£23.00	☐ Life	£510.00
☐ Under 25	£12.50	☐ Joint life	£730.00
☐ Family membership	£27.50	☐ Over-65 life	£300.00

I would like to make an additional gift of £

Total £

You can increase the value of your gift by 31.58% AT NO EXTRA COST TO YOURSELF. See overleaf.

I would like my subscription to help
CPRE's work in *(county of your choice)*

OR

☐ I do not wish to become a member, but wish to help
CPRE defend the countryside. Here is my donation of £

☐ I wish to pay by direct debit (see form overleaf)

☐ I enclose a cheque/PO made payable to CPRE

☐ I wish to pay by Access/Visa number

Card expiry date   Signature

☐ For a free summary of CPRE's policy recommendations on planning, environmental assessment, water, woodlands and forestry, transport, energy, agriculture, mining, landscape protection and other land-use issues, please tick here *(you do not need to join or donate to receive this)*

☐ I do not wish to receive mailings from other selected voluntary organisations

Code: 1025S

DIRECT DEBIT INSTRUCTION

Originator's identification number

7	2	4	2	4	5

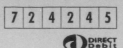

Bank _____

Full address of your branch _____

_____ Postcode _____

Name of account holder _____

Your bank account number

Your bank sort code number

YOUR INSTRUCTIONS TO THE BANK

Please pay CPRE Direct Debits from the account detailed on this instruction subject to the safeguards assured by the Direct Debit Scheme. (Copies of these safeguards are available from CPRE)

Signature(s) _____ Date _____

Banks and building societies may not accept Direct Debit instructions for some types of account

DEED OF COVENANT (TAX RECOVERY) FORM

To CPRE, I, (Name) _____

of (Address) _____

_____ Postcode _____

promise to pay you each year* such a sum as after deduction of income tax at the basic rate amounts to £_____ each year, or CPRE's current subscription, whichever is the greater.
(*enter the amount you will be giving CPRE annually*)

* The Inland Revenue requires that your power to stop making payments should not be exercised for at least four years (unless your death should occur sooner)

Signature _____

Date of signature _____

Ask a friend or relative to witness your signature

Witness' signature _____

Witness' name and address _____

_____ Postcode _____

You can give us the vital, long-term support we need to plan ahead by completing a direct debit. And if you yourself are a taxpayer, covenanting means you can increase the value of your gift by 31.58% at no extra cost to yourself. Just follow these 2 simple steps.

1. Complete the direct debit instruction telling your branch to make payments directly from your account, remembering to sign and date the form.

This allows CPRE to collect your subscription directly from your bank. It saves us money because we don't have to bother you with annual reminders, and your subscription can change without the need for a new mandate each time. We will always tell you in advance if we change your subscription, and you may cancel this authority at any time by advising us and your bank.

2. Complete the covenant (tax recovery) form. You will need to ask someone to witness and sign this form alongside you.

CPRE

Return completed forms to CPRE, FREEPOST, GOLDTHORPE, ROTHERHAM S63 9BR